Reviews

"Compelling tale of survival; I couldn't put it down…battles Katrina's deadly aftermath with invaluable tools: an incredible will to survive, a keen wit, and a pervasive sense of humor."
—Pat Leisner, former correspondent for The Associated Press

"Powerful. Klimitas's memoir captures the desperation and anxiety of a city held hostage by Hurricane Katrina."
—Jeff Moore, reporter for the *Daily Iberian*, New Iberia, Louisiana

"An amazing story. This is a stunningly clear account of one man's life in New Orleans after the floodwaters came. We're right there with him, savoring flash-backs to the people he has known over the years…the remembered closeness of his family…and the Robinson Crusoe-like challenges of satisfying life's basic needs in such a bleak environment. Best of all, it's a Katrina thriller with a happy ending."
—George Anders, author of the *New York Times* best-seller *Perfect Enough*

TWICE A SURVIVOR

TWICE A SURVIVOR

✦

A Katrina Journal

Hank Klimitas

iUniverse, Inc.
New York Lincoln Shanghai

TWICE A SURVIVOR
A Katrina Journal

iUniverse books may be ordered through booksellers or by contacting:

iUniverse
2021 Pine Lake Road, Suite 100
Lincoln, NE 68512
www.iuniverse.com
1-800-Authors (1-800-288-4677)

ISBN-13: 978-0-595-38191-3 (pbk)
ISBN-13: 978-0-595-82560-8 (ebk)
ISBN-10: 0-595-38191-X (pbk)
ISBN-10: 0-595-82560-5 (ebk)

Printed in the United States of America

For Adriana, Katherine, Judy, and Doug

Contents

Introduction 1

The Journal

Saturday, August 27, 2005 5

Sunday, August 28, 2005 6

Monday, August 29, 2005. 7

Tuesday, August 30, 2005. 12

Wednesday, August 31, 2005 17

Thursday, September 1, 2005 26

Friday, September 2, 2005 36

Saturday, September 3, 2005 45

Sunday, September 4, 2005. 53

Epilogue 59

Introduction

On August 28, 2005, a Category 5 hurricane was poised to hit New Orleans. I had time to evacuate, but even though my family had left, I decided to stay. Why?

I always maintained that I feared the locals more than I feared Mother Nature. Other hurricanes had come and gone over many years, most with little long-term effects. Our house was built over fifty years ago and never flooded. I never considered that the levees might not have been able to withstand a severe tidal surge. I felt that our house was strong enough to hold up under heavy winds, so my theories seemed reasonable. As it turned out, we didn't lose any shingles. At least I got that part right.

If I was wrong, I was prepared to stay for over a month on the second story of the house. I also knew my family in other parts of the state would come to get me if necessary. Unfortunately, Hurricane Katrina exceeded my expectations. Now I've learned my lesson. I've promised that I will evacuate if the need arises in the future.

While I was trapped for seven days, I needed to write. My wife still hasn't read what I've written; my daughter has only read segments. I hope that the readers of this journal will at least consider my viewpoint.

During my lifetime, I have had many successes and failures. When I had my double lung transplant, I was in the hospital for thirty-three days. I had to have a second surgery while there to repair an air leak that developed. It took over three months to get back on the road to recovery. This time, it will be an extended recovery also, but we will make it if we never give up.

The Journal

Saturday, August 27, 2005

Saturday, August 27 was a calm, warm day. Hurricane Katrina was in the Gulf of Mexico, heading toward New Orleans. Having moved here in 1989 from New Jersey, I had experienced bad weather, flooding, power outages, and the like before. I expected to have some problems but nothing that couldn't be overcome. This one would be tough, but I'm a survivor.

So far this year, we weathered Tropical Storm Cindy and Hurricane Dennis, which missed us. Our neighbor had evacuated for Hurricane Dennis. Somehow, he got pancreatitis while in Dallas and was still there, six weeks later. We have five dogs and a cat. Evacuation was not an uncomplicated event, and we were not anxious to move.

As daylight on Saturday drew to a close, the weathermen continuously urged evacuation because the storm was heading directly toward New Orleans. Winds were steadily increasing, making Katrina a Category 5 hurricane. That was bad. I dozed in my chair that night, watching the broadcasts. There was no sign of abatement or of the storm veering to either side of the Crescent City. Before my time, we had weathered Camille and Betsy; we should be all right.

My house was located next to a canal. I've always liked that because there were no neighbors across the street, only concrete. The neighbors I did have were quiet and friendly. My accountant lived two doors down. I rented out the house next door to a young couple with a child and one on the way. On the other side of me, college students occasionally practiced in a band-like fashion to notes I didn't recognize.

I'm a retired veterinarian. My wife, Adriana, still practices veterinary medicine. I assist her by being Mr. Mom. We have a child, Katherine, who has Brittle bone disorder and is in a wheelchair. Katherine's a junior at an advanced public high school. I live in Louisiana because my in-laws are great people and have always assisted us when we stumble. Oh, by the way, I'm fifty-eight years old and had a double lung transplant, but that's another story.

Sunday, August 28, 2005

At 3:00 AM Sunday, I got up from my chair and went into the bedroom to see if I could get my wife to evacuate. She said, "No, not now." She wanted to be wakened around 6:00 AM, so I waited. She wakened me at 7:30 AM to secure the office building. She did not return for three hours. In the meantime, I got my daughter up, and we started packing her things. The dogs seemed very calm. They had seen us pack before, and we always returned. Maybe they would come with us—that was a real treat.

Adriana returned around 11:00 AM and got herself together. We had done some preparation by filling the gas tanks; we had water and canned goods; and we put lots of ice in the freezers. My family—with the five dogs and a cat—left for New Iberia, Louisiana, where my in-laws live. They had a big house, but I knew they wouldn't be crazy about the animals. I hoped that Adriana would keep things under control. We talked by phone as she traveled there, and she arrived seven hours later (normal travel time is two and a half hours). At least they were safe. Adriana's sister was there too. She brought three dogs! I felt that I was in a good spot, not having to deal with the canine density.

By nightfall on Sunday, I became more concerned about the storm. I boxed up some food and picked out the critical papers from my files. I live in a camelback and have always liked the upstairs because you or a guest could disappear up there and come down when you had enough rest. There were two bedrooms and a full bath up there.

Winds were picking up in the evening. The storm was not losing intensity, and I figured that if everything was okay by noon Monday, I would be fine. That was my plan. The electricity failed at 5:00 AM.

Monday, August 29, 2005

Katrina hit with a lot of force. The trees were bending, my pine snapped in the backyard, and there was a lot of driving rain. The rain came in a window and under two doors downstairs, and I was continuously mopping up with towels. However, everything was under control. When the wind hit its peak, I moved my mattress and box spring to the front of the French doors, which overlook the backyard. They were backed up by my daughter's workbench and ceramics kiln. She is an artist.

When the winds were dissipating, I noticed that the backyard was filling from the back of the property with water. It was insidious. Well, I thought the pumps for New Orleans would take care of that. Unfortunately, it kept coming. I later found out that the pumps weren't going to be manned; therefore, they would not work.

The water kept coming and breached my doors in the early afternoon. I had moved all of my necessities to a counter by the stairwell. I had flashlights, rope, a cell phone, my checkbooks, important papers, two guns, a fan, a radio, and batteries. The bathtub was full of water and was holding. I thought I was set.

As the water came in, I started putting things up high; the dining room chairs went on the table, and the computer went upstairs. My beloved mixer—I was the family cook—was put on the counter. I transferred the large pot of ice from the freezer to the refrigerator. I put my daughter's dolls, which were given to her by paternal grandmother, on her large, four-poster bed (which once belonged to her maternal great-grandmother). I put shoes from the closets in bags and put them up high. I don't know where my wife got all those shoes. She always says that she has nothing to wear. I put my guitars up high on the bookshelves. When the water in the house was about a foot deep (I was wearing boots), I couldn't get around. I decided to move all of the packed boxes and necessities upstairs. I grabbed my daughter's bracelet to hold on to through what was coming.

I still had some things to put up, but I didn't expect the water to keep rising. At about 4:00 PM, in order to get around, I walked on two wicker chairs, placing one in front of the other to go forward. It was slow, but I had all of the time in the world—maybe. I put more stuff up, like the photo albums in the front foyer.

I grabbed two pots to help me distribute water upstairs. I found more papers. The water continued to rise to the point that I couldn't even get around on the chairs without getting water in my boots. Where are the pumps?

Nightfall came, and I listened to the radio. They were giving reports from people who had called in. My cell phone worked, but I wanted to conserve the power. I made a few calls to my in-laws. I recommended that my wife buy a new washer and dryer. I was glad everyone was safe. I had almost kept my favorite dog, Sasha, a Samoyed. Letting her go with them to New Iberia was the one bright change of mind that I had that day. I really like that dog.

My wife was concerned that I had no way to get to the roof. She was right. I hadn't brought a hammer or a hatchet, but I didn't tell her. I probably wouldn't be strong enough to hammer out anyway so I'd go out a window, if necessary.

So why was the water continuing to rise? The radio had no reports about why. I heard there was ten feet of water in the French Quarter, 770,000 people were without power, massive wind damage was prevalent south of I-10, and there was flooding north of I-10. There had to be a break in a levee somewhere. One lady had called in and said about four feet of water was rushing down Robert E. Lee Blvd, which was about a half mile from me on the lake (Pontchartrain). I wondered when the water would stop rising. I was upstairs, and I would look down the stairs to see how many steps were covered. As the water made the turn in the narrow staircase, I knew that I couldn't go down there again. What I had was what I needed to survive—prepared or not.

I had seen devastation before. When I was in veterinary practice, I had moved from a site only to have almost the entire block on which it was situated burn extensively. With fire, the materials are gone. With flood, there are some things that can be saved. I would find out what things I could save in time.

That night was calm again. Katrina had moved on to Hattiesburg, Mississippi, and beyond. Helicopters flew around at times and house alarms would go off. We had a freezer under the carport. Now the things in it, like the bread I had brought back from California, were floating around the backyard. So were the two heavy, wooden lawn chairs and some pots of flowers. Yesterday, I knew things were bad when the six-foot fence went under water. By Tuesday morning, the water would be up to the gutters on my home. I could no longer see my neighbor's car. The water was pretty dark. Welcome to the bayou.

The rising water stopped three steps from the top. I listened to a public official on the radio, who, when asked what the remaining residents should do now, responded by saying, "I told you so." He had no empathy, sympathy, or suggestions. What a jerk! I listened to the public officials talk about the power outages, curfews, rising water, and devastation. Hey, folks, tell me how to get rid of this water—that is step one. I think they avoided the issue because they didn't know. Shame on them. At that point, I hoped federal assistance would come up with a plan because the locals were in a quandary.

I worked out my plan. I figured I would be here for a month. Things had to last. I thought I would be all right. My home is six and a half feet below sea level; I have a little more water than that in my house. They talk about New Orleans being in a bowl. I reasoned that the bowl was filled. Only a heavy rain, and it was sunny now, would hurt my calculations. But the water was now level with the lake, so no waves please! It'll flow that way anyhow. I took consolation in that, and it made sense to me. It was better than the gloom and doom from the radio. And my phone was out, so it was the radio or nothing.

Northern view from 6622 Orleans Ave. August 30, 2005.

Southern view from 6622 Orleans Ave. August 30, 2005.

Tuesday, August 30, 2005

I started this project on Tuesday morning. There were a few books up here to read, but I'd like to record this event. I am essentially trapped, and the water is still outside. I could try for the roof, dangerous at the water's height right now, or I can sit it out. I have figured out my supplies for the month. I'd better eat the bananas soon. If we get another hurricane or even a tropical storm, I could be done for. I will survive. I'll make entries at least twice a day, and I'll walk two miles each day (forty feet from one bedroom to the other). I'll take my medicines. I'll try my cell once a day to reach my wife. I really love my family, and I'm sorry that I'm putting them through this. In time, I'll make it up to them, but probably not until October and beyond.

This afternoon, it is hot and still. The birds have come out; I hear them occasionally. I saw a mourning dove walking on the roof next door. I wonder if he saw me. As I look around, I review memories: walking my dogs in the area, watching my wife go off to work, taking my daughter to school. I wonder how much water they got. I worry about my wife's clinic because it is below sea level. Flood insurance was very high for that building; we didn't purchase any. This may not be the end of the world, but I can see the end of the world out of my second-story window. Planes continue to fly around at a swift, directed pace. I haven't seen any helicopters lately. I wonder why there haven't been any boaters. I am guessing with martial law declared and looting having taken place, no one is allowed out of their homes. The radio continues to admonish people about the impossibility of a quick return. They're right—return to what? I can't wait until the water goes down; I want to get back to work. I took a few pictures this morning. The camera died when I photographed myself in the mirror. I hope I get to process them. I'm going to read this afternoon; I've got to do something. I think I'm getting a headache.

They're marshalling flatboats to get people out. An airboat went down along the canal where the water has overrun the elevated (six feet) area. As for me, I'd be a hard one to move because I take all of these pills. I'm good for a couple of months. I have plenty of water. As I consume the water, I'll replace it from the tub, which is holding. They've finally mentioned the tsunami parallel on the radio. Like I've always maintained, man should be nice to his fellow man, and God will take care of the rest. This certainly is a challenge. My goal is to walk out my front door, look around, and start again. I hope my wife and daughter are not too distraught. I am giving them cause to worry. Life will go on.

They say the city is accumulating more water. The bowl is filling. Welcome to the club. All is static here except for that airboat's wake. They talked about boiling the water—with what? The water doesn't come out of the tap anyway. The depth of the water in the stairwell remains the same. I look down in it and visualize a nasty animal coming toward me, like a snake waiting there. It doesn't lash out; it just sits there beckoning me to challenge it. I don't. Perhaps I tantalize it. It hasn't got me, but it waits. It'll be waiting a long time. They just reported that it might be two months before we have electricity. That's a ways away. I can make it if I have to, but I'd better stretch my larder. It's a banana again for tonight's meal, with crackers. No lunch; just a glass of water.

The fellows on the radio are doing a tremendous job. Mayor Ray Nagin has finally come on and reviewed the disaster. He said that a two-to-three-block length of concrete in the Seventeenth Street canal is missing. Water is coming in there as well as in another area down in the Ninth Ward. A U.S. Army helicopter was bringing in 3,000-pound sandbags to stop the flow.

People are going to the Superdome. There are more sick folks. I don't want to be there; I'm not supposed to be in crowds. I like my aerie. Please keep working on those levee breaches. When the pumps start, the mayor said it will go down by one inch per hour. Let's see, that's a few days of pumping. And then we have the mud. Wow, what a challenge. The mayor said it will be two to four weeks for people to return. Let's see.

The mayor continued talking this afternoon. He recounted a story of eight to ten people who were rescued from an attic. One of the people said there was a little old lady in a neighboring house who was probably in her attic. The rescuers went to the house and removed the attic fan. She was there, smiling, and they got her out. What a story! I cried a little.

It's going to be hard to reestablish New Orleans. The main artery, I-10 East, was covered by the storm surge and moved. The span is now unsafe. The Causeway is structurally a question also. The swale at the railroad bridge at I-10, near the cemeteries, is filled with water. I don't know how many millions were spent on the new pumping station there, but it is inoperative. What a waste. So, if you can get around the cemetery area, you can go west on I-10. Gonzales, which is fifty miles away, has a safety area. Right now, my Toyota van is underwater. It is not a submarine. It probably won't operate again. It has 185,000 miles on it, only to end up like this. It seems unfair.

Seems like I'm writing a lot today. I guess there are a lot of thoughts crossing my mind. This is better than being in prison in that I have a number of amenities. I don't have running water, but the bed is great. Checked on the black murk in the stairwell—no change. There is even a little light down there from a horizontal window. Things have stopped falling. As the water rose, everything became buoyant. Loads shifted and down things would come. The sofas and my chair—my cozy recliner, my bed for many nights—are near the ceiling. They will sink soon. The dining room chairs, which I put up on the table, are now floating above the table. It's sad.

Here comes another airboat. As I sit here naked, I wonder how long it will be before I am discovered. I'll ask them for canned goods and leave it at that. I hate confrontations. Perhaps they will avoid me because I'm in the back half of the house and there are a lot of fences and wires.

It's now 3:00 PM, the height of the heat of the day. It's not bad in here, and I have a friend. A hornet is in the small room. That makes no sense, either.

4:30 PM—time for dinner: a banana, three unsalted crackers, some nuts, and a glass of water. A fellow could lose weight on this diet. Unfortunately, I'm not fat. I haven't been able to gain much weight since my surgery almost two years ago. Without the surgery, I wouldn't be here to experience this.

I made a great discovery: my wife has a toothbrush up here (and lots of toilet paper). Sometimes things work out. The water in the black hole (stairwell) is unchanged, and the choppers and planes occasionally fly over. People should be grateful for what they have. I feel like the Count of Monte Cristo, only at the Chateau d'If, the prison I don't understand how they had any ventilation in those dungeons.

I have taken a little nap and tried to visualize how we're going to clean up. I'll need water and my father-in-law's pressure washer. They'll have to pressure-wash me after this. I've only let my beard grow once (for two weeks), and it was itchy. Talk about forced obedience; I have no razor. Well, time to listen to the news again. They say my daughter will be out of school for ninety days. Catch-up is going to be hard.

It's now the evening of the first day after the hurricane hit. The five o'clock news reported that there is looting in the central business district. It would be hard to get after me because there are bars on the upstairs windows, which are not easily reachable. The previous owner put the bars there to prevent the teenagers from jumping into the pool. Now they protect me. The radio also said that Lakeview flooded because of the breach of the Seventeenth Street canal and that the water was rushing through the cemeteries. That's why the railroad bridge pump on I-10 would be to no avail even if it were working. They talk about bodies floating down in the Ninth Ward. I wonder how many will come from the cemeteries.

More on the looting: a policeman was shot in the head on General de Gaulle Drive. Who knows why? National television is showing the looting, with people taking goods in whatever they can put them in: cars, garbage cans, and bags. They are trying to set up a camp at Fort Polk to hold looters. What a shame; as Maestri[1] said, "We are on our knees trying to recover, and these people are taking advantage." Hope I don't have to shoot anyone.

Believe it or not, three fellows in a small boat with an outboard motor just went down our service road. They hailed at the rooftops, but I didn't answer. I was completing my mile walk for the night—sixty-five turns up and down the hall. A guy has to stay in shape. It is very still out there. Inside, I have closed the door to the stairwell and draped it with a bed cover. Who knows what scents will come from the murk. I have enough of that from the outside (minimal), and my bathroom, even though the door always stays shut. I am urinating in the toilet, but I don't dare flush it. Number two is in a large blue ice container, which I lean over. I cover both. My "last meal" before the ordeal was some homemade crab cakes. I didn't think they would survive. Now, obviously, nothing will.

This afternoon, I read about health—looks like I'll be eating more fish. I could have a line out the window now; but alas, I didn't bring one. All I would hook would be my bread. I'll never eat an artichoke loaf again without seeing it eight feet above my pool. It's still quiet; a few birds call here and there. The dog I heard for the last twenty-four hours no longer barks. Hope they got him out.

It's funny how things come into place by serendipity. I found an old *American Way* in the trash can from July of this year. Jessica Alba is featured. And the fantasies begin...about a night with her and my family and others in Miami. She sure is a good-looking gal. However, I have more than I can handle with my wife. We'll see if Alba is in as good a shape as Adriana when she is forty-two. When I get out of this, I'm going to help my wife more at the office (until she throws me out). Currently, I'm the lawn boy. Perhaps I can be elevated to go-for and then promoted again. Life has many promises for us. I think I'll get back to the health book; it should put me to sleep.

I had the radio on again. The Gretna city police chief said that the policeman who was shot would recover. The four perpetrators were apprehended (one shot).

---

1.   Walter Maestri, the Jefferson Parish director of emergency management

The police chief has received orders to do whatever is necessary to maintain order. He said that the dry dock from Bollinger Shipyard had broken loose during the storm, went two miles upriver, and pierced the side of a ship loaded with diesel fuel, spilling the fuel into the river. Then, the dry dock went back down the river and lodged in a levee but did not go through. The landing from the Gretna ferry just happened to land in the same place. Unbelievable!

I just tried to reach my family in New Iberia. The phone has no service. I feel for them because they worry about me. But, they know Dad is a tough guy. Girls, I love you.

The Harahan mayor described his situation on the radio. He was escorting people to their houses and escorting anyone else through the small city. He brought a "water buffalo" to the police station so that people can get drinking water (two gallons at a time). A councilwoman described how the pump trucks are working. I heard that the Southern Yacht Club had burned. I do have an extinguisher up here. It seems incredible that something could burn in the midst of that terrible storm. A lot of older people could not evacuate from Harahan; fortunately, they are all right.

There are more reports of destruction. The twin span of the I-10 to Slidell has large pieces missing. Plaquemine's Parish, south of here, has "been reclaimed by the river." We are still flooded. The only way out of the city is on the Crescent City Connection headed south. I am still resolute—or is that hardheaded? It is now hotter than at anytime today. I can visualize the air-conditioning. I am thinking about my daughter, watching *Wheel of Fortune* and *Full House*. I would be looking forward to *Law and Order*. I would be making dinner. Those days will be back—I guarantee!

A caller on the radio just described his tough situation. He was in a senior citizen's complex, and he needed oxygenation and a CPAP machine. He has sleep apnea. He had a twelve-ounce bottle of water, no food, and is a diabetic. He is looking for help for himself as well as for the other twenty or so at his complex. He is very close to a hospital but can't move. All he can do is report the problem. Sad.

For me, life is getting better. I found my glasses. Nightfall will bring cooler weather. I have my water. I have my life. Tonight I should be playing basketball. I am though, in my mind. I scored a few points and the team won. I am a happy person in my mind. I've got to combat anxiety. I must go on.

Wednesday, August 31, 2005

It was a quiet night; I only got up once. The helicopters have resumed work. I turned on the radio, and it was disheartening. They said that the water is rising in the city. It's not rising here. The broadcasters were trying to help a family at Carrollton and Earhart by telling them to get on the roof. The water was rising there, and now it is at six feet. What happened to me is now happening around the city. The key is to plug up the levees. Hope they're working on that. They're asking people to go to expressways so they can be picked up. How can the people who were around here get down there? It's sad. Who's first—women and children? I once again affirm my intention to walk out of here. The radio just stopped broadcasting; I'm gonna check it. It's going to be a hot one today. I'm in a holding pattern.

The local radio station, 1350, doesn't work anymore. I picked up a Baton Rouge station, 1210, which is normally a news/sports station. Got a stock market report and some guy wondering about the Saints' home games. I'm going to do my morning routine. Be back. Oh, something's burning outside. Why? Glad I've got my extinguisher.

I found a news station—1150, out of Baton Rouge. A lot of state offices are closed. One lady mentioned that Lake Pontchartrain has a two-foot elevation and because the Seventeenth Street canal is not repaired, the water may continue to rise until the levels are equal in both area. Hmmm—if it rises two feet, I'm still okay, I've got three stair steps. The water outside is at the top of the glass of the French doors. The burning smell has gone away. A hamburger would taste good about now.

After an inventory of my supplies, I got some bad news. The apples are starting to rot. Got the worst one out and ate the best parts. I don't want to expand my stomach much, so it's getting used to minimum intake. The only thing in good shape is fluid. I've got three large bottles of water plus soda. Think I'll drink some Sprite and do my morning walk.

The governor has come on the radio. It's a prayer broadcast. Archbishop Hughes followed. This is a day of prayer, and he said, "God has brought us to our knees in the face of the destruction…we don't know how to respond…powerlessness leads us to prayer." He then quoted St. Paul's letter to the Romans, saying,

"We know that all things work for good for those who love God." I turned the radio off. Is God responsible for this? Why pray? Sometimes, you're on your own. You may get lucky, and we make our own luck. Sometimes, we exercise bad judgment, i.e., like my staying, but I'm working with what I've got. I'll stick with Winston Churchill: "Never, never, never, never, never, never, never…give up!"

The plan for today is to sit tight. The outlying parishes are starting to recover. It's like attacking a problem by nibbling away at various sides. In a couple of weeks, they'll be ready for the core and that's me. I'll walk out the front door; hopefully to Adriana and her dad. Still no phone service today. Gonna be hot.

When I was growing up in New Jersey on a farm, we had no air-conditioning. I had the upstairs room. It faced north and west, so it was the hottest in summer and the coldest in winter. This room faces north and south. Actually, that's good in that the sun doesn't come pouring in here. See, another good point.

It's only 10:00 AM, and I'm sweating just sitting here. I hold my daughter's bracelet for a moment for good luck.

It's 11:00 AM. Another boat just went down the service road. Looks like they had water—two large blue chests in the boat. I let them go by. I'm sure there are other folks who need it more. I have my northerly window open by six inches, but it would be somewhat hard to tell I'm here since I have the bars on them with semiopaque, white curtains. I have two southerly windows open, one in the bathroom for obvious reasons (I call it the outhouse), and the other over my bed, which I shifted against the southerly wall. It has a wooden shutter on the house side of it. If people would wonder why they were open, they'd have to figure that someone was in there. You wouldn't leave the windows open for a hurricane. I hope that people with unfavorable reasons don't think I am protecting something, like cash, jewelry, food, water, etc. We'll see. Time for my other half of a can of sirloin burger and country vegetable. Have you ever noticed how all of the peas sink to the bottom of the can? Eating from a can is nothing for me; I've done it all my life. I especially like Chef Boyardee Ravioli. When they changed their recipe, I went to Campbell's Chunky material. Oh well. I could use a case of that Chef Boyardee right now and not be picky.

I don't want to waste any water, but it's hard to get it to the glass from a large jug. What I do is pour some into a pot with a handle and then transfer to a glass. Now I don't waste a drop. In time, the water in the bathtub may not be good. I'll transfer it into an empty bottle if I get to that point, but I'm not sure how that will keep it from spoiling further. There's got to be germs in the air especially since the "outhouse" is in the same room as the bathtub. Both waste receptacles are covered with towels to minimize the germs; there's not much else I can do.

The faucet lets air out of it. I do have some water in the bowl in the back of the toilet as a last resort. Hopefully, it will get to be flushed down normally in time.

I'm able to write this memoir because I found a loose-leaf binder in the closet up here. It was called the *History of the Klimitas Family*. It mainly centered on my maternal grandparents because my mom saved some early items, like a passport to and from Hungary in the 1930s. There was a lot of paper in the back of the collection and that is what I'm using. Frankly, along with the radio, it keeps me occupied and keeps me from going mad. I wonder how incarcerated people handle it. It would be easy to give up. For me it would be even easier—I have a gun.

I just read a letter to the editor in that *American Way* magazine about how a frequent flyer exchanged his first class seat with a soldier returning to the States. Good for him! I served for two and a half years but did not have any combat duty. I am now experiencing, probably in a better way, the entrapment and loneliness our boys experience in Iraq. I am convinced that you can't change people. I don't see the point in wasting American lives for the sake of establishing democracy worldwide. If there is a problem, let's just pull out and utilize technology. Satellites pinpoint the target; bombs do the rest. What about innocent lives? Well, are they really innocent when the kids are the product of their parents? Their parents believe in Allah, and they pass it on. Look at World War II. Hiroshima got their attention; pinpoint bombing should be enough.

There was a caller into the radio station that didn't want to evacuate because he had a dog. You could hear it in the background. He was told that he couldn't bring it to the Superdome. He had twelve ounces of water left, and his home was still surrounded by water. It was time to leave. I don't know how I would have handled that.

I miss my dogs. I visualize taking them for a walk, sometimes a pull (when they go after a cat), and a stop and sniff. Sniffing was a big thing to them. They wanted to know who had traversed their neighborhood. All of my dogs were female so they didn't have to mark every tree on the block. But they had to check out the new scents—reading the animal telegraph along the way. Most of the dogs we encountered barked at them. Some stared. I hope that they all are safe. I guess I'm still a veterinarian at heart.

Oh boy, lunch. Two Triscuit crackers, six nuts, and a glass of water (and served on the water, what could be better?).

Here comes a helicopter that is closer than any of the others that have passed over. Must be looking for someone in particular. It actually hovered over the intersection of Orleans and Porteous at a level of five stories up. I look at the other houses; no windows seem to be open. The trees are like matchsticks; some are broken, some leaning. The oak in front of my neighbor's looks like a lady who just got out of bed with disheveled hair. But no major pieces are broken. I love the oaks; they're majestic and deserve respect because of their age. I hear that the oaks on St. Charles Avenue did not fair well.

This reminds me of when we lived in Florida. At one point, I had 120 orange trees and one grapefruit tree. Then we had an extremely bad winter. I lost half of them. I used a chain saw on the dead ones and had an open burning. I thought I was okay. The next winter, there was another cold spell. I lost the rest except for the one that was protected by the house. I hope we don't get another Katrina, but I think that in time, it will occur. As to what I do in the meantime, I'm not sure. I always said I would die here, but hey it's not time to go yet. Back to reading.

This afternoon, it is very still. The leaves are not moving. It is hot. I lie naked in the bed only to get up and wipe the sweat from my body. Sounds like another airboat coming up the canal. They sure make a lot of noise (and wake). This one, it turns out, is going down Marshall Haig. He's gone, but his wake can be seen as a minor undulation of the water outside my window—otherwise known as the swamp. More stuff has surfaced. Little stuff, like a can of paint, a few boards, and a can of WD40. The chairs have disappeared. The large plastic chest with our pool gear lingers in the corner. We had a plan to empty the backyard of water via the pool emptying to the street. A minor plan for a major catastrophe. This shows how susceptible New Orleans is to devastation. We could be immobilized by two or three breaks in the right place along the canals. Mother Nature, as we have seen, will do the rest.

Good and bad news this afternoon from the radio. Lake Pontchartrain is equalized and some of the water is actually going out. I think that's right. The level on the French doors seems to be down an inch or two. This also has allowed them to work on the breaks in the canals. They dropped seventeen large concrete blocks into the breach, but I understand the breach is two and a half city blocks long. It's a start. They talk about economics. One lady wondered where her check on the first would be. First of October would be more like it. My wife's business will not be up and running for a month, if then. I hope she's not vandalized. There were two cockatiels left there; I wonder if they'll make it.

I have to say this: the radio has been great in giving certain perspectives, but the one person who is outstanding in giving information and hope is the mayor, Ray Nagin. Good for you.

1:30 PM. The newsmen are making the point that until 4:00 PM Friday, we were not in the cone of error; the predictions of a Florida/Alabama landfall were not good. In the final analysis, weathermen can show what is and then give their best guess. They guessed wrong. No surprise there. They are paid to continue to predict. They are ex-stockbrokers.

I miss my family and hope that they won't be too mad at me when we see each other. They are predicting thirty days before the water is out. Now people are on the overpasses. The sun is out in full force. They are evacuating the hospitals. My mom got out of the hospital Friday. She went back to her nursing home, which evacuated Saturday. She dodged a bullet. All of her things are in a small room at the home on a second story, inner floor. I have some paperwork of hers. Currently, it is about three feet under water in a filing cabinet. I'll be doing a lot of drying of papers.

As I lie here, I think about a scene in the 1973 movie *Papillon* where the prisoner is told to conserve his energy because he's going to need it. Now, there was a survival movie. Steve McQueen always was incorrigible, a tough guy. Once again, I'm being asked how tough I am. We'll see. They're moving 23,000 people from the Superdome. They're not going to worry about me. They're taking them out in buses. I've always hated buses since I had to ride public transportation through high school. It was always full, and when I got on, some "cool" kids would light up in the back, and I'd be standing there. But, in time, folks would get off. And I'd get to sit. And I'd get home. Life was structured and loving.

They're going to be letting people into Jefferson Parish on Monday, which would be September 5. I wonder how my wife's clinic is. It is near the Lakeside Mall, which is at Veterans and Causeway, about one mile from Lake Pontchartrain. Her area is low and would flood, but her building had not flooded as far back as 1980. This is a new era. What's good for her is that they must have the pumps running out there, and she is not in the "bowl," which has quickly changed to the "bowel."

I hope when she comes that they don't get the idea to bring a boat and try to get in here to rescue me. That would be too dangerous. But we'll see. If the shoe were on the other foot, I'd probably try it if I could get past the authorities. And if I couldn't, I'd wait for nightfall. I've been watching too many war movies. After all this isn't a Navy Seal operation.

It's 2:30 PM, and I've just walked another mile. My ice pack with my insulin is gone, so I'm going to make it without it the rest of the way. So I don't strain my pancreas, I'll spread out the meals to snacks. My barber, Ray, is a diabetic, but he doesn't take insulin. He walks five miles a day; so far he is controlled. I'll have to limit the sodas, and start spreading them out too. If I get woozy, I'll have to use the insulin. It can survive in a cool place. The trouble is, there is no cool place. I towel off some more sweat. I listen to a few voices; they're off in the distance (to the north), but the sound carries very well over the water.

Just had a quarter of a glass of water. My deliveryman said there were three gallons in the containers when filled to a line on the lower neck of the bottle. If they're filled to the brim, there's more. He had given me full bottles. I am thankful for the little courtesy.

The afternoon is hot, and the choppers are flying over, it seems like every ten minutes. There is a lot of activity. I wonder again about reconstruction. I don't think that the water is high enough to reach my ceilings. Next door, it is very close. My afternoon snack is five nuts and a Capri Sun. There are some clouds out there, and it probably dropped the temperature a few degrees. I still sweat when I lie down though. There is no breeze.

They're talking about the folks on the overpass again on the radio. They are on the elevated areas of I-10. There is no drinking water or food. The National Guard is at the Superdome, which is a marshalling area, and they will be distributing supplies from there. People can get the basics. They keep talking about ice as a basic. I don't get that—it's nice, but it doesn't beat water, crackers, and canned goods. They're asking that people get up on the roofs, yet there are stories about people being passed up. There will be federal aid. They are busing around 20,000 people to the Houston Astrodome. It will take several days.

Oliver Thomas[1] told a story about a couple. The woman was pregnant, stranded on the interstate in the east. The car had given out, and while there was flood water behind and in front of them, railroad tankers were flipped on the road near them, trapping them. A policeman picked them up and took them to the Superdome. I hope she's okay. What a way to start a family.

The radio is featuring various public officials. I hear a lot of stories. There have been a lot of bodies in the water. People have had to leave them, yet the picture of a person floating remains in their minds. Quite an image. The water is starting to go down in Jefferson Parish. They're looting again. They said that there seemed to be a horde of people ready to go out and steal as soon as the storm passed through. They tell a story about people stealing postal trucks using AK-47s and looting stores. If they have to be shot, it's time to send a message. The federal government is supplying various teams. They have even sent a hospital ship. The president said, "We're working on stopping the water." They say it'll be thirty days. And so I go with the September plan. I'll be here until the end of Septem-

---

1.   New Orleans City Council president

ber. I will say this: there are *more* helicopters now. I haven't felt this way since 9/11. President Bush, "May God bless you."

Another councilman, Chris Roberts, said that across the river in Terrytown, people were being held at gunpoint in their own homes. The police are haggard and running low on fuel. I hope the National Guard will control this.

With regard to looting, I'll be sleeping with my pistols. I guess it's better to be sitting in seven feet of water. My God, not only is it the swamp, it's also a moat!

Dinnertime: one banana, two Darvocet pills, and water. It isn't Commanders, but it'll do.

The radio transmission is going well. The speaker said that we are working in an extremely primitive condition. She ranted about the plight of the people who decided, for whatever reason, to stay. Rhetoric is cheap; it's nice to hear. She said we're going to restore law and order. This is a primitive state, and they must shoot the nefarious element. Being a forgiving person is akin to getting yourself killed. So, if we shoot looters, that'll start to solve the problem. They also announced that the general in charge of dumping the sandbags decided not to do it at this time. Once again, the key to this is getting rid of the water. Forget the rhetoric—stop the water. My comment to the general is to ask why. On the broadcast, they also told the story about how the residents of the local prison ended up on the Broad Street Bridge and then were escorted out of town (probably moved 2,100 now; 3,000 to go). They take them up to the railroad bridge on I-10 by boat. Then they are distributed around the state. Wow!

Hey, good news. One gentleman just announced that a contractor is coming tomorrow to set up a large driver and start driving pilings in the area of the breached levee. He was only on a minute, said his bit, and got off. Thank you, we need doers. They said people would get angry, disoriented, and saddened. It's true. You feel all emotions from the deepest parts of your mind.

An educator has come on to urge people to get their kids enrolled in any school possible. I hope Adriana heard this. I think that Katherine could possibly fit in at the Episcopal School near Lafayette. I sure appreciate my in-laws now. They had their camp on Vermillion Bay destroyed by Hurricane Lilly. They rebuilt it better than it was. So, we have a precedent in the family for rebuilding. They can guide us. We do need help (besides—inside joke—my father-in-law has all my tools).

They are calling this the worst natural disaster to ever hit the United States. I agree. The president is bringing in a lot of help. He said that the response of the nation will be overwhelming. I hope so.

The people who need supplies and stayed at home in Jefferson Parish will be given help at distribution points. (I hope that they aren't followed back to their homes and pillaged.) Wal-Mart is supporting this—remind me to buy that stock. And, the Gumbo Crew has been set up with Whole Foods to produce meals. They will start tomorrow. All of this was announced through WWL-AM. I'm amazed at the response!

I think about how I was when I first came here. One time, my family evacuated, but I stayed behind and slept on a raft in my clinic. I feared the locals more than the weather. If I were there now, I would be four to eight feet above the linoleum…in a raft! I guess my supplies would be on a shelf. It would be a lot hotter because it was a closed, middle space with only two doors. The windows were totally barred. Here, at least, I can open the windows. Still, there is very little breeze. Very little!

It's evening and getting a little hard to see. A couple of weeks ago, sunrise was at 6:30 AM and sundown was at 7:30 PM. I'm sure the days have gotten a little shorter. I feel like Amos Moses, in song, a man of the swamp. We're starting to get a little scum on the water, which makes it look more forbidding and not fresh like it is out in the true swamp. But I don't have duckweed. Another figure of literature I think about is Robinson Crusoe. He had an island and a dog, as I recall. I have a lily pad: a wall-to-wall green carpet. You can't always get what you want, but you get what you need.

I forget if I mentioned that I have a small fan, a Porta Breeze. It takes D batteries, and I didn't have spares. The radio takes AA, and I have two packages of those. The radio is much more important than the fan. Mr. Towel is filling in. I figure I won't have a shower for a month. When I had my surgery, I didn't shave for about twelve days. I will be El Grubbo, but that's okay. I have set up a small stepladder with a container of rocks by my bed. If someone evil approaches, I can kick it over as I reach for the gun under the pillow. Again, I've been watching too many movies. Right, Clint?

My affairs are in pretty good order. I paid the house notes and my mom's nursing bill is paid for September. I have my neighbor's mail (at least his bills). I'm not sure about what to do regarding the rent for the house next door. Frankly, the place will need rebuilding. Their lease is up in January 2006, but they wanted to renew for a year. Nothing is in writing.

It may be unwise to sell. I think the housing value here will definitely drop; after all, who wants swamp property? It really depends on how tough the locals are. One person on the radio said that they had enough and were going to move away. The commentator stated that a number of retail businesses would take this as a cue to move their headquarters, just as Hibernia Bank, which was recently bought by Chase, decided to do. I don't blame them. What's the old saying? Fool me once, shame on you; fool me twice, shame on me. No one can predict the future, but one can have vision. I think I'll focus on the upbeat message of Mayor Nagin and forge on. By the way, Ray, have you seen Noah pass by?

Almost dark; hope the temperature drops the routine ten degrees. It'll be a tough night if it doesn't. In here, it's cooler to move around slowly than to sit. Now I know why orangutans move about with their arms held out—they're hot and they're airing out their armpits! When I put my arms over my head in bed, it's not real pleasant. What a day.

More on the Gumbo Crew. They are setting up in Norco, and guess what? The firefighters are coming down from New York to assist. I am impressed and grateful. People are saying that 1.3 million people were displaced and that the problems are astronomical. Our culture is affected—the United States is affected. The newscasters project the area won't be functional for a month or two. I think not. The United States is mobilized.

One funny thing about this—I live in Lakeview. Gee, I see the lake just outside my window. I've always wanted waterfront property!

Thursday, September 1, 2005

What a night. It was very still and, as the commentator had predicted, you could see the stars. I never really cared. That was something you did in the islands with your mate. Well, it was clear, but, of course, I wished that it wasn't. This is like being at war: destruction all around, short supplies, wondering about your loved ones, little communication, and no conveniences.

The radio commentators keep asking people on the radio why they stayed. These people are looking for help. I think the question should be if you stayed, why weren't you prepared? There's a segment of society that expects the United States to provide a basic level of sustenance to which they can fall back on so they won't go any further sustaining their own life. They don't have to think on their own. These people are now in serious trouble. If they stayed put, they have no water or food. If they went out, they're on a bridge somewhere with no place to sleep. It's strange that even prisoners get better service.

This morning, I had an apple for breakfast—not bad; it keeps the system moving. The water in the tub is maintaining, so I wiped myself off with a washrag several times. I even brushed my teeth with water only. Adriana has all types of bath materials up here but no bar soap, no toothpaste, and no dental floss. I found a toothpick in my valise. I'll manage.

I have another visitor—a salamander. It's about two inches long, brownish-gray, and sleek. I put an empty can of sirloin burger on its side with water in it for him/her. Hope he makes it. Hope he doesn't bring friends. Last night, the frogs were very active, especially one about fifty feet from my southerly window.

The water level has gone down, believe it or not. It is now one foot from the top of the French doors. Is that a sign? Well, it's a step in the right direction. The birds call (crows mostly) and the helicopters fly. It's 9:30 AM. I hold my daughter's bracelet again as well as my ring. Will New Orleans rise again? In time, in time.

Just finished my walk. Arms akimbo, I traverse my two rooms and hall. It's still cooler to walk than to sit. I put some crackers down for the salamander, which I named Ed, but he has disappeared. I wonder what his plan is. The water is like glass, it's so still. The twenty-foot maple tree next door has leaned over our fence and is starting to die. The leaves are shriveling—what a waste. I like trees. Personally, I've only seen destruction like this when my mom and I visited England some years back after a hurricane had flattened everything. You put years into a project, your life, your surroundings, and it's gone in an instant. Very sad.

We had quite an extensive hurricane in New Jersey when I was a kid. Hurricane Hazel caved in our shed, and we were without power for a week. We cooked on a pit made of cinder blocks and got our water from a lake two miles down the road. We transported it in a fifty-five-gallon drum. For us kids, it was an adventure. The main difference here is the flooding; we'd be much better off without it.

No service again with the phone. I'll try again tomorrow. I feel like a tiger in a cage; the walk was mesmerizing. I see a magnificent animal walking back and forth. I see me walking. I'm not magnificent by any means, but my freedom too is curtailed. Yes, I could walk out in a manner of speaking but, after considering the options, I'm choosing to wait. A slight breeze has come up. Now it's time for the radio.

They reported on the radio that a shot was fired at a helicopter helping with the evacuation at the Superdome. They are going to take 25,000 people to San Antonio. Many are afraid of a rush on the buses. As the folks in the Superdome are setting up for rescue, others are coming from the surrounding areas. That could be instant panic. A lady has called in from 2911 First Street, between Willow and Claiborne. She has six children. She is asking for food and water since they ran out yesterday. Boats going by are ignoring them. The radio personalities are in Baton Rouge; they have taken the message. Hopefully, the rescue people will find them before it's too late. On top of everything else, there are ants and mosquitoes in the home too.

Rosalie from Algiers called in. She represents three or four families in a section where there is no water on the streets. She has some drinking water. Her request was for some ice and a generator. She has gas in her car. The authorities won't let her drive out. Obviously, they have a phone. Her sister now has asked for lights because their home has not sustained serious damage. Tina must work for WII-FM.

Great news! Metairie is no longer flooded. Now, I wonder about the looting. I'm sure it will happen there—they're taking shoes, sporting goods, and guns; they broke into JC Penney. Hopefully, they won't burn anything.

A lady named Denise called in from a Jackson and Magazine location. The dead body sitting outside her door has been there for three days. She has a niece who brought her some supplies. She describes old people sitting around in the park. There is no running water. The broadcasters wonder about cholera and dysentery. Again, let's get rid of this water. She wants to stay put, but people know she has supplies. She is subject to anarchy because when nightfall comes, there is no law. I sleep with both guns under my pillow. Now, they're reporting a gang carjacked supplies headed to a hospital.

A rescue person has just reported that this area, Canal/Robert E. Lee/Harrison, has been canvassed. They're saying it was eight to ten feet from where Interstate 610 hits Canal Street. At the top of Canal Street, it was only two or three feet deep. NOMA has water up to the steps, though I'm not sure which ones. Tad Gormley Stadium was full of water like a bowl of cereal. I just checked my depth gauge, but my pool cabinet has partly obstructed the view. The water is definitely down about a foot. The sky is overcast, but they're predicting temperatures in the mid-90s again today.

An interesting commentary has been going around about staying in New Orleans, now that the worst-case scenario has occurred. They said that after 9/11, New York would see an exodus. It didn't happen. Will New Orleans fare as well as New York? I hope so, but it will be very difficult. I hope I get to see it.

I went to sleep for about three hours. It is cooler, and I'm not lying there sweating away like last night. Planes and choppers have slowed down, and no one has come by in boats. Time for lunch—some crackers and nuts. Then back to the radio probably. There is a lot more rumbling in the distance; we should get showers. My French doors are once again exposed, and I think the water has gone down another two inches.

My wife has a stationary punching bag with a water base I could hardly move prior to the storm. It is now located in our neighbor's yard. I can now see my neighbor's (to the south, the rental) back fence. The moveable gate in front of the back driveway is floating up. The large pine trees (thirty to forty feet) on the next street are all leaning at about thirty degrees to the south. One had already started leaning prior to the storm, and I figured it would cause us to lose our electricity. One night, when I took the dogs out, they treed an opossum up one of the pines. I wonder where that opossum is now? That was about six months ago, during late winter. It's funny how all of these memories come filtering back. I have had a lot to be grateful for, and I will continue to be grateful. A chopper flies low to the north.

I have three jugs of water. How much would I sell one of them for? The answer is that they are not for sale. This is the hand that I have been dealt. I do not wish to make a profit, and I do not wish to help anyone. If there was someone else here, even a friend or a relative, I would be confrontational. Fortunately, I made my own hand, and I will take the consequences. Unfortunately for my fellow man, I am a loner; I can't help him anyway.

The radio reports that some officers, twenty-three deputies, and Sheriff Phil Miller have come down from Douglas County, Georgia. The city of Gretna has asked people to stay on the Greater New Orleans Bridge because there is nothing that can be done for these folks in Jefferson Parish. That means that there is no way to walk out of the city. You have to stay near the Superdome and get picked up by the buses. At the end of a previous call, an officer with a voice like Ice-T was on saying that the National Guard was not well-deployed. I wonder what that means.

If I have written this before, I apologize. Why did I stay? Because I worked too hard to get this far, and if something was going to happen to take this away, I wanted to be present to minimize the effect. True, I could have packed what I saved in my van, and I wouldn't have this uncertainty. But who knew? I didn't realize that the levees could only withstand a Category 3 hurricane and fail with a Category 5. If I knew that, I would have moved out. I feel for the couple who bought my practice. My wife should be okay. I didn't want to move because my daughter could go to Benjamin Franklin High School if she was in Orleans Parish. It was the top public high school in Louisiana, and she was doing well there. I also liked being here because it's close to Ochsner Hospital, where I had surgery awhile back. Life was, I guess, too good. Boy, my beard itches.

The lawlessness continues. Four thousand National Guard are here. There was a riot and lockdown in Baton Rouge (all from the New Orleans influx). There will be 12,000 National Guard soldiers here by tomorrow. Some shelters have space, some don't. If these people had radios, they might know where to go. Governor Blanco is going to get 40,000 troops. Wow! This is a shame. It's starting to rain little, tiny droplets. Somehow, I know how Davey Crockett felt, although his demise was a certainty. I think I can wait long enough for the "bad guys" to be cleared out.

I want to talk about some good memories that I have. My wife, daughter, her cousin, and I took a short but exceptional Carnival Cruise trip to Mexico. Yeah, I could see the stars in the night sky, and I could hold my wife for as long as I wanted. My daughter and her cousin, Emily, would do their own thing, having figured out how to traverse the ship (remember, my daughter is in a wheelchair). We had walkie-talkies. One time she said, "Dad, hurry up and get down here. They won't let me claim my prize—a bottle of champagne for bingo." She was a minor, so we got it exchanged. We ate great; there were no cares. Life was good. I can't live the good life, but once in a while, I get to experience it.

I remember my wedding day. We had a small ceremony and a small reception (300 people). My wife looked great. I had to be in town, coming from New Jersey, for less than twenty-four hours. I even met my in-laws for the first time. I lived minimally in Jersey, and my mother-in-law referred to my lair as the inn of the cave-bear. I wasn't exactly what she expected for a son-in-law.

I remember my daughter's eighth grade play, *Annie*. She had a few bit parts in it. I can still see her zipping across a darkened stage with a flashlight. My dog, Sasha, was in it too. Both got flowers afterward, and Sasha liked hers because they were from the Three Dog Bakery.

When I had my lung transplant in October 2003, I spent about a month in the hospital. I was in despair on the fifth day after I regained consciousness, wondering if I'd make it out alive. I was unconscious for a week. I called my friend, Rick, in South Carolina. Rick was a physician and methodically went over any physical signs and symptoms, and said I should be okay. He told me he would be down the next day. He stuck by his word—now that's a friend. I set a goal after my surgery to see my daughter graduate from high school. One out of four patients don't make it through their first year after surgery. I will succeed in reaching my goal and more.

I went to the bathroom. I've got advice for Johnson & Johnson: if you put your old banana peels and apple cores in a basket in the bathroom, they help negate the scent of the waste material in the area.

Garland Robinette has just blamed FEMA and the president for not being able to come to Louisiana's aid right away. He wonders where the C-rations, water, and law enforcement are. He said that this situation was known for years and asked why we weren't ready. Could it be that such a pronouncement would hamper the local economy? Could it be why a number of large businesses have relocated? *Laissez le bon temps roule*, or in English, "let the good times roll." The smart people were out of the bowl. But there were people, like me, who made a personal choice to stay, and we needed rescuing too. How could these officials tell me there were no more supplies? It has only been four days! No one has taken personal responsibility for anything here. It's only poor me. People like Garland Robinette foster the idea that someone should take care of everyone without any effort on their part. He said the head of FEMA should be fired. I say Garland should be demoted to sweeping floors. He said we are at war and I agree, but his inflammatory remarks only serve to justify irresponsibility. He should be grateful instead of awful.

It's 2:24 PM, and Garland Robinette is back on his pedestal. He is responding to a lady calling from Breaux Bridge. She says she is worried about her family on the West Bank. There is no law. The Oakwood Mall is burning. These people moved to the West Bank from New Orleans. The radio says that there are also hordes of people still at the Superdome. It will take a lot of buses to move them. They're saying that it will take weeks to get electricity in Folsom, and that's forty miles from here. I am preparing for the long haul.

What they *should* be broadcasting is that looters will not be tolerated and that they will be shot. There's no other answer. Are they afraid of violating someone's civil rights? These people are the dregs of society.

I went for my afternoon walk—half a mile in the pacing area. Again, I feel like a tiger. That's part of how they stay in shape. I tried to organize my thoughts and let the bile level go down a la Robinette. I hope that his shift is over soon. Last night, I remembered one thing I read in a book about Buffalo Bill. Now if you were a plainsman, you took a lot of chances, especially running with those buffalo. At one point, Bill broke his leg and couldn't get back to civilization. So he and his friend set the leg. He stayed in a shelter while his buddy went back and promised to return with help. Talk about angst. Suppose his friend was killed along the way. Well, they were reunited and Buffalo Bill added to his legend.

Call me Lakeview Hank. I'm sending a message through the skies telepathically to my father-in-law. Doug, bring a boat with you—a flat-bottomed one—to Metairie. Launch it and come get me. Approach from the southern side and come up the service alley. Shout out my name so I don't shoot you. It's okay if you bring Adriana, but no one else except a law enforcement officer if they insist. I'm okay; I'm okay; I'm waiting. End of message.

Lunch—five filberts, five Ritz crackers, and two swigs of water.

I used to have a dog named Tamburlane. He was an Afghan hound. A nice dog but very dumb. I heard they cloned an Afghan hound recently; it's probably easier to do because they have fewer brain cells. The only breed that has approached this level of mental density in my lifetime is the Italian Greyhound. Anyway, Tamburlane developed kidney disease and needed a special diet. The diet consisted of a dry portion and a wet portion, and all the ingredients came from the grocery store. One ingredient was chicken noodle soup. Well, he was on the diet for two years or more, and I'd prepare it, taking a nip of the soup. To this day, however, I hate chicken noodle soup. Today I have these crackers. Most of them are low in sodium because my daughter has some pulmonary hypertension. If I make it through, I will never have a low-sodium cracker again.

One of the radio fellows made a funny remark. He said that the gas in his car's tank is worth more than his car, which is completely submerged. They're saying how this storm will affect the gas supply along the eastern seaboard. Guess so, but there are a number of refineries in Philadelphia, so it should stop there. It continues to rain and be hot.

They report that power is on at the New Orleans airport. This is very good in that it would be a receiving area for aid. It will also bring in more security troops.

The director of FEMA, Mike Brown, has come on the radio and rebutted the failings of the initial response of the governments to the disaster. I have no TV but he reflects on people screaming into the camera as just another time for them to grandstand. They have said that the bodies, which are thousands, will be taken to St. Gabriel. I'm not sure where that is. He has brought up the problem of disease, saying that it may not necessarily be a big problem. Good answer. He points out that the Superdome area continues to attract more people. He emphasizes that the distribution of food and water is continuing. If someone refuses to move and thus hampers the cleanup of the area, they will be forcibly removed. Some people now refuse to go. I feel for them. They have an attachment to their homes. People are starting to suffer from heat exhaustion and mental fatigue. I understand; it's hard enough without anyone around.

Garland Robinette is back on. He has criticized the FEMA director for saying that the violence is under control. Supposedly, men with AK-47s have tried to break into the Children's Hospital (it probably did not happen). Gunshots have been fired from the bridge at the firemen fighting the Oakwood Mall fire. Robinette is now off the soapbox. Let's analyze this. What types of people are left? Are they bright, are they workers, do they have a trade? Can they do anything besides eat? Okay. Now these people are foisted onto other communities who are expected to absorb them out of the goodness of their hearts. Sounds like a big problem with no good solution.

The phone calls continue. Here's a lady on the phone with a baby, three small children, and five adults. They have water but no food. Their house had three floors; the roof came off in the storm. It rained today, and the second floor bedroom accumulated water, causing the kitchen ceiling to fall. She was given telephone numbers to call.

A fellow called refuting Garland Robinette's trashing of the federal government. He states that the locals have not adequately prepared themselves and are shifting responsibility. Fortunately, Robinette is giving him time to talk. The caller makes the point that the president cannot declare martial law without the governor's request. He blames the local authorities for the shortfalls. He wonders why the locals could not arrange to protect the gun stores. Robinette continues to rant about the fact that we supply 25 percent of the nation's fuel, and it has been totally disrupted. Really? There was a report of no significant damage to any chemical plant.

Toyota has determined that it will donate $5 million to a relief fund. Good for them. Louisiana is not underwater. Hey, my Toyota is underwater. I still love that van. They're talking about not having many clothes. All of mine are underwater. Fortunately, I can walk around in the buff without any sensitivity. When I was recovering in the hospital, I used to inadvertently moon the steelworkers at my window. After a while, one has no couth.

Karen from the American Red Cross is giving a report. They have given out many meals. This is their largest effort ever. Now Jesse Jackson has come on. Does this guy ever miss an opportunity to be seen? Let's see what he says. He asked that folks not panic and coordinate with each other—I hope the folks are paying attention. He is asking for the churches to open their houses and hearts, saying, "We must turn to each other, not turn on each other." He is going to Xavier to get students out. Hey, he does have a plan, albeit a small plan, to help. Good for him. "Though it is dark, the morning cometh." This is testing our faith, he said, and urged churches to cooperate. He asked that we focus on the people, not the looting.

The newscasters on the radio said that a politician, whose name I missed, questioned rebuilding New Orleans because it's below sea level. What's the point? That means that the two houses I have in New Orleans are essentially worthless. Can I walk away? I did it once before in my life. I took all that I had and put it into a VW Rabbit with two cats. It's tougher now that I have a family, but it will get better. People are calling for debt relief. Wow, I think we're going back to the depression in a way.

Another caller has phoned in from the East. She felt safe in her house. She would rather stay inside where she can hear the gunshots rather than go outside and see the gunshots. (Great quote, Melissa Hughes.) There is water up to her doorstep and plenty in the street. Dump trucks are going up and down the street. They will take you to Chef Menteur Highway for $10 or $20. I guess they have to cover their gas. The commentator also talked about going through Tickfaw and guess what, a lot of roads were clear. The citizens had gotten out and cleared them without any federal, state, or local assistance. I smiled. I think about my dad. He had his job as a chemical engineer, but he loved his independence. And we survived on the farm. Hey, Pops. Are you watching me? I'm thinking about you.

"We're here to help you and this is how you repay us?" said a lady from St. Charles Avenue, which normally has little crime. Now someone was carjacked at a hospital, cars were being broken into, and a school had its computers stolen. I think that the locals have taken the opportunity to commit crimes, operating under a diversion where others can be blamed. I hope when my family comes, they keep one person with the vehicle with a gun while the others come to get me.

It's time for a banana, which is extremely ripe. Dinner—*bon appetit*! (I leave a little for Ed.)

Aaron Broussard is locking down Jefferson Parish. There will be armed officers at the east and west border. At 5:45 PM, the parish shuts down. He is acting as if this is a foreign country. He did not get the federal troops. Good for him. He said he couldn't bring people in to repair things if they're going to be shot. He will take peoples' lives to enforce this dictum. "As of five minutes ago, we're going back to the Old West. Mr. President, are you getting this? I've gone from a president to a dictator. I'm running like this because you have abandoned me." Sheriff Harry Lee asks where the water is. The staging area is I-10 and Causeway. Parish President Aaron Broussard said, "Nero is fiddling as Rome is burning." He means Nero is Bush.

It's 6:00 PM. Garland Robinette is done his shift—now that's a ray of sunshine. Deke Bellavia has taken over. A reporter, David Blake, said that the Superdome is surrounded by three to four feet of water. The space between the New Orleans Center and the Superdome is completely filled with people. They have a loudspeaker system going to reassure the people. The crowds have thinned a little. They are still crushed up against each other. Others are on the overpass and out in the sun. These folks have gotten something to eat and drink. As soon as the large masses are gone, it will free up the guards to do other things.

A frustrated black lady from Pearl River who lived in New Orleans is on. She said that there was an element that shouldn't have been allowed to exist: the crime. She said that they have to be controlled. With all the do-gooders, how can we do this? For me, this reminds me of Castro sending us his trash as we allowed the Cubans to relocate.

I am now listening to Ray Nagin's speech from two hours ago. "Excuse my French, I am pissed," he said. Nagin needs 500 buses; he needs troops. He stated that the Feds are thinking too small. People are in their attics up to their necks and dying. Nagin called for martial law two days ago for New Orleans. Drug addicts are looking for a fix; they find guns; and they are wreaking havoc. He is forming a perimeter around the heavy drug areas. "I probably don't want to deal with me after this is all over. I want a moratorium on press conferences. Get up off your asses and do something to fix the biggest goddamn crisis we ever had. People are dying! They don't have homes, they don't have jobs. The city of New

Orleans will never be the same," he said. The mayor broke down and cried. End of interview.

Nagin mentioned that they talked about fixing the Seventeenth Street levee. They talked about the sandbags and containers. Guess what? Nothing has been done for two days. Please *do* something.

Another lady called in about St. Bernard Parish. Some people went from St. Bernard on a boat to Baton Rouge. They were told to go to Vicksburg. Shouldn't they go further north? I guess they've run out of gas.

Good news! A lady called in. She is on I-55, heading south from Memphis. Several convoys are headed this way. I hope that they'll be here soon. I guess they'll go to that staging area at Causeway and Veterans. Michael from Charity Hospital said that the massive exodus has finally started. He feels that Louisianans will rebuild. Four people died there last night. This fellow was the husband of someone who worked at the hospital. He didn't even have to be there. He wants the president of the City Council, who is in Baton Rouge, to be in New Orleans and not be a government in exile. Well said.

I'll have to sign off for the night. The sound carries very well over the water, and I want to hear them before they see me. Ed has shown up again. Don't have much to offer him. One time, when I was in a self-imposed exile, I had a spider plant. Her name was Susie. It's funny where and how you find small comforts. Deke made the point about the media copters coming in. The crowd thinks they'll be helped, but they're only photographed. Sad.

Friday, September 2, 2005

Slept in this morning; it wasn't as sweltering as the night before. I forgot to mention it, but a small boat was out around 8:15 PM last night, after dark. They were shining a light down on Porteous. I figured it must have been teenagers. Last night, it was again very still. That frog was active though, not the cat.

At night, I think about things I'd like to say the next day or whenever I can remember to put them into writing. Since this is a diary/chronicle, I'm allowed to incorporate any ideas. I liked *Tuesdays with Morrie* in that it made you think about your life. Morrie was slipping; I hope I am not. It's best sleeping in the early hours. After dark, I open the long, sliding glass window to make it look the same as if it was closed. I close it at daybreak and go back to sleep. Frankly, it's not the crows that wake me up because the helicopters are running all the time; the crows sound off in the morning.

I thought about the close calls here in New Orleans, times when my own or my wife's life was threatened. I must have been known as a nutcase at our business. At one point, I tackled one of four high school fellows who came into our shop and proceeded to run out with merchandise. That's how I met Police Sergeant Curry, a World War II veteran who was a local town fixture. He gave me much advice after that. One time, my wife was a victim of a smash-and-grab robbery on St. Charles and Calliope at 1:00 AM. And on another night I was accosted when I went home late. I backed against the wall on the street and this fellow, who was in much better shape than I, had a standoff with me. He asked for money, but I knew that as soon as I got my money out, he would grab it. We both just stood there outside each other's reach. We talked—finally he ran off.

Another time, we had a flood and all of us ended up at the local bar. When one of my workers stood up after many hours of drinking (and the waters had receded), she fell backward and hit her head on the pool table. Another fellow offered to help me carry her to the car. As we were going down the street, he tried to pick my pocket. I was going to deck him, or at least try, when the other female coworker intervened and talked him down while I took Denise the rest of the way. The last time, I had moved to my new hospital and was checking on some animals at 10:00 PM (fire victims, but that's another story), and two young thugs approached me on bicycles. One played sentry, the other tried to knock my block off. Fortunately, I kept him on one side of a swinging gate, just out of reach, while I called him every name in the book at the top of my lungs. They went away. At that point, my lungs were so bad that if they had hung in there another half a minute, I would have probably collapsed. But they didn't know that.

I'm sure there are more stories as my memory recollects. I always viewed myself living in New Orleans as a cowboy. Now, as before, I have come to the conclusion that if I have to shoot someone, I will. I was always impressed by the number of women that carried guns when I got here in 1989. That was life in the big city. I'd rather be facing an inquiry than the gates of wherever.

Yesterday, the Oakwood Mall burned because of vandals. About ten years ago, a large distribution center in the East burned because, I think, of a disgruntled employee. The place, from which I moved my veterinary practice, burned (almost a city block) due to arson, but it was never proven. Incidentally, the police thought they had the culprit and then suddenly the main witness was killed (was the word on the street). Tough town. The point I want to make is that those last two burned areas were rebuilt. I guess it's like California and the earthquake. People respond to the challenge. This time we just need a stronger levee system.

Last night, my restless leg syndrome kept on occurring—must be from drinking soda. I figure I'll move the soda (which I'm long on) drinking to the morning so that the tendency wears off, and I can rest without moving all around and twitching my legs. Some nights it got so bad, I would sit in front of the TV, without it being on, so that my wife could rest. Then, I'd serve her breakfast in bed come morning.

Today's going to be a big day—I'm going to have some tuna, and I'm not going to pour off and waste the juice. There is no service on the cell phone this morning; I'm turning it off.

Good news, we are down another six inches. That's great because that gives more air circulation so that the ceilings don't collapse. I wonder why the drop? I didn't hear of any action yesterday on the levees. Two things that I like to hear each day are the weather forecast and the levee report. We'll see. No sign of Ed yet, although I'm not out looking for him.

I continue to listen to the radio. Spud McConnell, WWL news commentator, just lost it on a caller who, initially giving good information on Web sites and blogs, began to criticize the Iraqi war. "This was no time," Spud said, "to voice your opinion about that." And he refused to waste the airtime. He apologized for his outburst; I laughed and applauded him. The news on the radio reported a blast and burning building down on Poydras near Canal. I don't hear anything, and I don't see any smoke.

When the hurricane was at its peak, I thought I smelled gas in the laundry room. I turned off the heater. The other one is located in the attic to my east. If the first heater goes, I'm sitting right over it. That could be the ball game. This whole thing is turning into a mind game. I think about miners trapped in coalmines (my grandfather was a miner). The news also mention a siege and dead school children in Russia (yesterday was the one-year anniversary); I think of Spencer Tracy in *Devil at 4 O' Clock*. All of these miseries—what is going to happen to me? What is going to happen? Once again, I am grateful that my family and the dogs are safe.

I'm thinking about my wife's business. They are describing how the streets will be littered with trees. Well, I thought there were no trees around her until I remembered the two-and-a-half-story sycamore that is one story away from her building on the north side. All the trees around here bend south. I never liked that tree. I hope that it broke apart rather than fall over.

"My Lord and my God, I do not know what will happen to me this day. I commend myself into your hands with complete trust. Amen." Parish President Broussard just gave this prayer. Good thought. He commented on the possibility of bulldozing New Orleans. He talked about the historic greatness. Evidently, New Orleans burned in the 1700s. Only the Ursuline Convent survived because it was surrounded by a wall. He talked about other disasters and recoveries. Can you believe it—he was dressed in LSU colors. What a guy!

The rhetoric continues. This will be done, these people are coming, and we have these plans. As I've always said, I would rather deal with a total jerk who got things done than a yes-man who doesn't get the job done in a timely manner. Fifteen thousand people were evacuated from the Superdome last night. About 5,000 are still waiting. There should be a few more trying to make it to the Dome. Everyone is running out of supplies.

10:00 AM—company! The Hotards, our former neighbors, have come to look at their parents' house. I hear them after they dock their boat at the back garage and climb on the roof. They successfully knock out a second window and go in to take out two large plastic containers of cherished items. There's Jane and four or five fellows. So, why am I still here? I could have gone out with them. I could at least have gotten out the word, even if I didn't go. I guess I'm paranoid. As long as no one knows I'm here, I feel safe for some reason. If I went out with them, I couldn't bring all that I wanted and had no way of continuing on once I got to wherever their base of operations is. Once again, my stubbornness and thinking are definitely questionable. I'm going to make this. I hope those broken windows don't give anybody ideas. The nights will be longer. This was definitely a fork in the road.

Guess what? I found a bar of Dove soap in the shower. Things are looking up. Time for my morning walk.

I think a lot on the walk. Back and forth, back and forth. I'm not a big guy, 145 pounds at the height of the storm, 5'11", and round shouldered. When I had my transplant, I was 135 pounds, having gone up from 128 pounds when I finally sold my practice. I was a veterinarian with a genetic lung disease. After the surgery, I went down to as low as 117 pounds. The day I weighed less than my wife was a bad day. At that time, I had a lot of problems with medications. Empirically, I took between thirty and forty pills a day. After three months, I decided to find out what made my stomach churn. For a long time, all I would eat was wonton soup. People would come over and bring other stuff, especially Florence, an older Italian lady who, I'm sure, weathered out the storm in Folsom. Iron was my main problem. That pill made me sick regardless of the type of iron it contained. I reduced my other medication intake and gradually got better.

Then I started to get a lot of headaches. That proved to be mostly a dietary thing. Any booze whatsoever, any chocolate, and any uncooked milk products would give me trouble two to four hours later. This morning, I put some water on a plate I found for Ed to soak his skin in. As my reward, there was an old Kit Kat bar from Halloween in the same drawer. But chocolate is a no-no even in these dire times. As for my weight, I went as high as 157 pounds and felt good enough to start playing basketball. It dropped, though, when I had to stop playing because I broke my foot (kicked a doorjamb) and broke a rib. (I was inadvertently smashed from behind in a game.) I learned that it takes three to four weeks to mend those cracks and every night during that time would be painful. I was supposed to have a checkup at Ochsner Hospital yesterday; I'm sure they didn't miss me. I hope they're well. By the way, all of my monitoring devices are underwater, but I'm in good shape on pills.

Lunch: two swigs of Coke, one-half can of tuna (albacore), four crackers, five nuts, and one swig of water.

I am listening to a replay of Mayor Nagin's interview. He talked about the politicians just spinning. He said, "BS—where's the beef? Where is the help? Where are the ships? They—the federal government—are thinking small. There are still people in their attics up to their necks. The looters got control for a while because law enforcement was being used to save people." At the end of the speech, both Nagin and Garland Robinette (the interviewer) cried.

A huge convoy is now on Route 90 and coming across the Greater New Orleans Bridge (GNO). Finally—can you believe this—they have declared martial law and have orders to shoot to kill looters. About time! It is unacceptable to condone these people. They are giving other news, stating that October 19 is the start of Saddam's trial. That's my birthday. Hope I get to see it.

Let me say this: the reason I am sitting here is to prove to people that you can take care of yourself, you can prepare, you can face a worst-case scenario, and you can sacrifice. You can survive. Let this be a testament to that. Am I right? There are many sides, but I am committed.

It's 12:30 PM. The president is working his way across the Gulf Coast. He is now in Biloxi and will be at the New Orleans airport this afternoon. East Jefferson Hospital, which is about a mile from my wife's clinic, is asking for personnel to return. After all, the people who served the less fortunate in the hospital have been there for five days. They need relief. They can also be reassured that it is safe because the National Guard and the local police are there. Another caller salutes Radio 870, WWL, for staying on the air. I agree, the individual personalities have been very concerned, levelheaded, and noninflammatory (except for Garland Robinette's rancor, but he made you think, which he likes to do). Time for a nap.

At 2:00 PM, I am awakened by almost incessant helicopter activity. They are flying constantly; one almost buzzed the house. I sharpen my eyeballs and ascertain that the bank of earth between my street (Orleans Avenue) and the built-up levee is visible. I see grass! And it looks green! I am encouraged. For me, it was a major event when I mowed my lawn after my surgery. I hadn't done it for almost six years prior to that because my emphysema was getting so bad. After my surgery, people commented about how my color got better. One client said, "Gee, doc, I thought you were dead." I think they'll get to say that to me again.

Went for my afternoon walk—half a mile. Again, it is cooler to walk than to sit on the bed and write. The sun is out. I am toweling off with various pieces of cloth. Thought about other survivors, like *The Old Man and the Sea*. My skin puts out a few more droplets in response. Thought of another war story about a fellow on an island in the Pacific during World War II. He was there by himself and, as I, feared the locals (Japanese) more than the elements. He transmitted information to the American troops and was finally rescued.

As far as the looters go, I am encouraged with the water dropping. That makes it more difficult to navigate with all the detritus and submerged objects. It also is tougher to reach my window. That gives me a little more time in case of an encroachment.

Here's another memory. One of my clients—I'll call him Bob—was moving his household goods from one location to another by himself. This was about ten years ago, uptown. He had cats. After a hard day, he lay down in a back room and pulled the door shut. Many houses there are called shotguns because they are long and narrow. Or maybe that's so you could shoot your wife's lover as he was exiting out the back. Anyway, at night, he heard a noise and thought it was the cats. He heard another noise, getting closer, and he audibly loaded his 9mm pistol. Then he peered under the door (In the old houses, doors had a lot of clearance from the floor for ventilation.) and there were a pair of boots coming his way. He leaned back and sprayed the door. One of the bullets caught the guy in the femoral artery. He bled to death about a block away. His accomplice was eventually sentenced to a long prison term.

When the police came to the scene, they confiscated the gun. He said, "Wait a minute. Suppose the robber's buddy comes back, then what?" No one cared. The next day, he went into Orleans Parish, and no one would sell him a gun after they heard his story. He went to Metairie, Jefferson Parish. The fellow listened to his story and said, "Ten percent off any gun here, extra ammunition, and a year's free membership in the gun club!" Bob stayed in town for a little while, but he wasn't exactly blessed. One afternoon, the neighbors saw his car being put on a tow truck. They thought it needed work. Well, no, someone was stealing it. He left the town soon afterward. I wish him good luck still.

Good news! I found a few Q-tips. My daughter is always asking me for them for her ears. And it's better than putting my sweaty finger in that area. They are playing Mayor Nagin's interview speech again. He said, "Whenever you mention that you're from New Orleans, everybody's eyes light up." That's true. I have had to do a bit of traveling since my operation, mainly to California, and all one hears is about the great times they had while in our city. The people, the food. When a friend from California visited a couple of months back, the first thing I did was to take him for brunch to the Court of Two Sisters. That was a highlight for him. We also visited Kliebert's Alligator Farm, after lunch at Middendorf's.

I wonder if Middendorf's in Manchac is still there. It was on low-lying land at the western end of the lake. My mouth waters when I think of their fried catfish. If I were living near the gator farm, I would wonder about escapees, although they had stragglers come into their area from the swamp. Still, lots of small stuff plus 150 gators (breeders) that had been there since 1947. Fortunately, I don't see anything moving my way outside. Yikes!

Three hospitals are open: East Jeff, West Jeff, and my friends at Ochsner. They are asking for relief, and safety has been guaranteed. Great news. A lady is looking for Madeline Morris. She lived in Lakeview but evacuated, I guess, to the Holiday Inn on Loyola downtown. No one knows where she is. Water and food have arrived and people are feeling better. I don't know how they have made it so far in the hot sun. They're reporting that some places are charging $4 a gallon for gasoline. When they've got you by the balls, the hearts and minds will follow. I've never found an answer for the gas problem. I guess all I can do is get a smaller car and make it a hybrid, even if they aren't fully developed. They're reporting that Saddam may be facing the death penalty. It's been a year since we found him cringing in a hole; once again, "swift" justice is cranking along.

The commentators are waiting for the president to make a statement at the airport. He has been in meetings with the mayor, U.S. Senators, and other elected officials. All have criticized him. They say that there are still people caught in attics. Now let me see, why are they there? It's because the water is still there. Get rid of the water, and we can walk out. Seems like this idea is being ignored.

I want to hear about that levee. Close it off. As these building and trees stand in the water, they will weaken. Give me a break! When can we start the pumps? I have a shirt that says, "New Orleans. It's not the heat, it's the stupidity." Please show me I'm wrong. The president and the mayor are taking an aerial tour of New Orleans to review the devastation. I look out my southerly window and see two very strong-looking gray helicopters flying over the canal right now. I can't help but think it's them. I salute them, and I hope that they get my point telepathically about the water level. This is a great country. Let's see some great things.

The reports for the last hour are basically people trying to locate individuals. Without our ever-present cell phones, locating people has proved to be almost impossible. I just try mine once a day so I don't run down the battery. They also talk about a fellow in the east who was trapped in his house and wouldn't be rescued. They called him a paranoid schizophrenic because he had to be hauled out kicking and screaming. I'm going to reason with the rescuers and ask for the Sagreras to get me. That should satisfy any of them. I just hope the Sagreras are not too unhappy with me. I've caused them a lot of angst.

The head of Brown's Dairy in New Orleans called in. He reported that a number of his trucks were stolen. The plant is down on Carondelet south of Route 90. One of the trucks ended up in Houston. He needs to coordinate with his other plants in Shreveport to service the hospitals. He needs a letter to retrieve equipment and then, I assume, come back in and deliver milk. All of those trucks have to be emptied. Violence, stench, and heat have taken its toll. The commentators say that we have a $10 billion relief bill ready to be signed. They report that the stock market has finished lower. They say that oil reserves have been released. Stopgap measures are coming out at a rapid rate. People will have to realize that they will have to work to make it. And that means more than forty hours a week. I wonder. Some folks are just so used to being on the dole, why should they change?

Starting at 6:00 AM on Monday, September 5, Labor Day, people will be allowed to get into Jefferson Parish, get their stuff, and get out. A lady said that she knows that her loved ones are at 3320 Edenborn. They won't let her into her parish until Monday. She has food and water but no power. She wants to go get them now because all they have at this point are chips. I'm surprised she can still communicate with them. It's rough to be able to help and not be allowed to.

It had to happen, Chantrell called in with a very good idea. She said she believes that there will be plenty of jobs. There are plenty of jobs for contractors, roofers, etc., people just need to get ready. Then she went on praying to God. I just shook my head. The commentators agreed with her though. They talked about the effect on tourism. They said that the zoo is in pretty good shape. They talked about historical sites. Speaking of historical sites, I remember going to the St. Louis Cathedral to hear a Christmas concert. The acoustics were incredible. I hope I can relive that moment in the future.

Deke said that they are broadcasting to thirty-eight states at night. Bad news. It will take eleven weeks to get the water out (that's eighty days). They stated that the sandbags are just engulfed by the water. That makes one pause. I wonder why it will take so long. I've got to believe that it just won't be that long.

I just listened to the president's speech after he toured the city. The one important thing he said was that they are working unceasingly to fill the break in the Seventeenth Street canal with both federal and state help. He said it would be thirty-six to eighty days for dry land here in the bowl. I've got to believe in the lower number. Maybe I'll see it, maybe I won't. I will put together the most important things in case I have to evacuate before that time. I have enough water. Food is the issue. I believe you can go nine or ten days without food but only two to three days without water before serious consequences. I was taught that a person needs at least thirty milliliters per pound body weight per day to survive. I'm much under that. I really don't want to make a thorough analysis at this time even though I have a calculator.

It's 5:15 PM and dead calm. I've been pretty verbose today. I'll stop here and get a few nuts for dinner. I'll do some reading. As Durante used to say, "Good night Mrs. New Orleans, wherever you are."

Or maybe I won't. Cancel the nuts, garçon. It's 7:10 PM, near sundown. Bring on the Ritz—crackers, unsalted, six. I could use some pâté. Checked out the water situation, at my current rate of use, I have a minimum of forty days. I also found my "frozen" bar for my insulin. No longer useful, *au contraire*, it contains water, I think. Put that idea as last ditch. I also separated all of my papers to the essentials, birth certificates, mortgage agreements, etc. and have them in a bag ready to go. Without food or water, I think I'm allowed two carry-ons, both of which can fit under the seat in front of me. The other box has my medications and enough room for a gun. If I'm going to make a run for the border, I'd better be able to defend myself. I have a few bucks in my wallet, not that there's an open 7-Eleven down the road. But I figure as time goes on, the area of devastation around New Orleans to the west will shrink, and I can walk out if Sagrera, Ltd. or the troopers haven't rescued me.

So, again, why am I doing this? Why don't I start waving at the helicopters? I fear that they can't complete my mission, which is to get to New Iberia. At least for now. Why do men climb mountains? Why do men abandon their families for a job? Why are there some who willingly go to Iraq? We all have our reasons. It is a challenge. I hope my ordeal will show others that you can succeed with seemingly very little. It's going to be a hot one again tonight. I'll listen to a little more radio transmission, and then wait to hear that frog.

It's still Friday night. I don't want to turn on a flashlight, but I want to make some comments. They said that people would be allowed to enter Jefferson Parish at 6:00 AM. What a stampede that should be. I hope that Sagrera Ltd. figures out a way to get around it. I'm not going to count on them, but I can hope. The caller makes the point that New Orleans is in a social state, that there is a class that depends totally on the government. Garland Robinette said that these people should be dispersed. Sounds like Section Eight. The only problem is, who wants to live by them? If they moved in next to me, I'd have to make some serious decisions. They are saying that it will not come back as it was. I think they're right; it may be time to move. I'm running out of daylight. The final point is that educated people do tend to make a decent wage.

Saturday, September 3, 2005

What a night. It was still, it was hot. Nothing moved. The cat cried initially, then nothing. There was one chopper hovering over the school (Haynes to the south) and then at approximately Argonne and Chapelle (to the north). Not sure what he was doing; he didn't come down very low. I had to turn on the radio twice as well as the fan to beat the heat. I had taken two Darvocets. The best time is between 2:00 AM and 8:00 AM. There is a coolness that comes. I like to see the leaves moving a little, at least. It is a psychological comfort in itself. The water level is the same—one and a half feet from the top of the glass of the French door. The maple tree leaves have died. They will fall soon. I hope that the authorities realize that all these trees will die. What a shame. It will become suburbia, which I always disliked. The homes will have to be bulldozed.

When I redid an old double on Magazine Street, the beams were made of cypress. They might make it; the other woods, I'm not so sure. The metals will be gone. We just got in a new air conditioner. Hey, Mike, it's not working! Where will all of this trash go? I don't hear any crows this morning.

I had awakened this morning about 8:00 AM, caught a little news, and then went into my routine. I've got soda out in a cup to lose its carbonation. I drink some of that and some water and eat a few nuts. The last banana is starting to rot. I discard a quarter of it and eat the rest. I go for my mile walk, and it sharpens my mind. I do my morning constitutional. When I traveled a long time ago, in Turkey, you had no commode. It was a hole in the floor. Guess you had to get pretty good with your aim. I have a large trough-like receptacle, which I cover. It's okay, but you can't crouch there for long, no musing or reading the journals, as I was prone to do. I washed my hands and that felt good. I wonder how long the water will stay fresh in the tub. Looks okay now, and the level is still holding.

One time, my wife and I went to a bed-and-breakfast in St. Vincent. It was my only experience with a waterbed. It did tend to stay cool, and I could use that right now. We went out in a pirogue, and I was a little scared. She was a pro. I'll never forget switching positions; I thought I would tip it over. But I didn't. Once I calmed down, I got to view nature and the bayou. I'm doing it again.

I thought again about why I'm doing this. Basically, I fought too hard to get what I have to just walk away. I walked away with $10 from my first wife, was scarred forever, and got nothing when she subsequently became a millionaire. I don't want to walk away again, not without a fight. This time, I'm dealing with Mother Nature, not a human. Yes, and Mother Nature is a mother. Frankly, I'd rather deal with her than a human. Hey, the choppers are flying again. Should I moon them? This is my fourth day without clothes. At least I have no additional laundry, and my electric bill is down.

The latest report on the Seventeenth Street levee is that they almost have it filled in. Pumping station Number 6 has to be made dry, and then they have to check out its generators. They feel that they will be no good and are flying in replacements. They are damming up and drying out the canal to accomplish all of this. Seven days until they start pumping, thirty-six days until the water is out. Jefferson Parish is letting owners into the parish as of Monday and then the three days after that, it can be anyone. I hope that Sagrera Ltd. uses that as a staging area and sees fit to get me. If not, I'm basing everything I do on moving out on October 1, 2005. I am optimistic, but, hey, things are coming along. Now if I could only get a little breeze.

I wonder how Joanne is. She was my right-hand person when I ran my clinic. We saw a lot of cats and did a lot of surgery. She had about twenty cats and lived in a shotgun double near the cemeteries. When I heard that cat last night, I thought of her. Here's a prayer for you and yours.

The mayor of Kenner has announced the times for the Masses of Our Lady of Perpetual Help. The return for 6:00 AM Monday is still on, but please do not stay. There are two spots for the distribution of water and food—one is on Loyola and the other on Esplanade—and they are sponsored by Wal-Mart. Thank you, Wal-Mart, you have been spectacular. The commentators talk about finding places to live. They say that Algiers is in pretty good shape, but there are thousands of people who need food. The area is clear, but the security is minimal. Troops after dark do not exist. She talks about people who could have left, but did not want to leave their dogs. This lady, Alexandra, has put up signs that she will shoot first and ask questions later. She also has two attack pit bulls. Chris Miller said, "Hey, normally I'd be afraid of her but, in these circumstances, you'd probably want her in your foxhole." Amen.

Jefferson Parish wants you to bring only cash and gas. You must go back out. You can come down I-55 to Airline Road and then come in or on the east side of River Road. I-10 is restricted to military personnel and evacuations. Entergy reports 9,600 workers on the ground. They are not working in Plaquemines,

Orleans, or St. Bernard Parishes. At the height of the storm, 800,000 were out of electricity. Now about 270,000 have restored power. The circle is tightening. This is very good. As an aside, my initial set of batteries in my radio still is working. Amazing. Thank you, Eveready.

It's 11:00 AM. There are three guys, all in camouflage, driving an airboat down Orleans Avenue. They must be hot. Right idea, wrong bus. I still don't like the option of putting myself out there and not having a clear path to New Iberia. Besides, you can't hear much with that motor's noise. I let them pass. The water is still again and getting darker.

My daughter is a kick. She's a chip off the old block. Recently, we sent mail to our displaced neighbor (the fellow with pancreatitis in Dallas). She included a card that had a picture of our lawn on our front and said we rally miss him since he hasn't been mowing the grass. Yes, I do miss Brad and Tara. These young peoples' lives shouldn't be so complicated. My daughter left with some of her books. I hope she's well and not too frustrated about not hearing from me. She will, she will. I've got to write these affirmations each day to keep up my spirits, and it does help.

So David Vitter has come on the radio. He said that touring is good because he doesn't believe anything that he doesn't see with his own eyes. He viewed Oakwood Mall, which, he pointed out to an aide, the water, fire, and vandalism/ destruction did not come from a hurricane. He felt that the West Bank is in better shape than the East and that Gretna is very orderly. They need supplies. The news has come on. Four thousand active-duty troopers are here and 7,000 more will come in seventy-two hours. Saks on Canal Place is burning and so are some warehouses down near the waterfront. The trash at New Orleans Arena is everywhere with very little clean areas. They stopped picking up people at the Dome and are now concentrating on the Civic Center. People are dying at a triage center at the airport. You know, you can get safe water by melting ice cubes. Hmmm, now to find the ice! My wife had four freezers of meat, the rest being at New Orleans Cold Storage. I wonder how that is. It was pointed out that they are letting the fire at the warehouse in the Bywater burn itself out.

A lady has called in asking how the cemeteries have faired. She knew that some of her relations were in St. Vincent de Paul Cemetery Number 3 but wasn't sure of the exact location. Why didn't she know, and why the concern now? As for me, my mom and I are each going to be cremated. I have a contract with Bultman at Louisiana and St. Charles. Hope they come back, and I better not die now as they're going to be plenty busy for a while. The commentators talk about the Cities of the Dead as in *Easy Rider*. They wonder how you will be able to tell the difference in a recently dead person versus one out of a grave. How macabre!

The head of St. Bernard Parish, Larry Garrigiola, has reported in. The National Guard has come, but they need supplies. There is only a small area on St. Bernard Highway and Paris Road that is dry. Ninety-five percent of the houses are destroyed or underwater. He asks that no one return for weeks or months. He called out on a cell phone; he was heartbroken. There is no reason to stay.

The governor has come on the radio. General Honore will coordinate efforts. Mr. Witt, former head of FEMA, has been hired to advise. They point out that 20,000 people were evacuated from the Superdome yesterday. All of the hospitals have been evacuated (except for East Jeff, West Jeff, Ochsner, and a few at Lindy Boggs). The fire is at 101 Pryor Street Wharf. A lot of reports coming in are false. Generators are heading to Mandeville and Covington. The people who are still being evacuated have to go further away (forty-seven are going to Arkansas). They talk about the missing kids; how could that ever happen? These are children they are taking care of. Fortunately, only about twenty-six kids were evacuated for medical reasons, with parents not allowed to go. Otherwise, there was some pushing when getting on the buses.

The Florida Baptist Church in Baton Rouge is acting as a service point. The pastor, Pastor Trammel, has come on and said they are serving 16,000 meals per day. They have a health unit. They have eighteen-wheelers with supplies. They are serving as a center for donations. They will have services tomorrow. They are doing something to help their fellow man. Quite an organization!

I have lunch: five Triscuits, six nuts, a small cup of Sprite, and a swig of water. I can feel my stomach shrinking. It doesn't hurt, and I must keep it moving. I'm not going to stop eating, but I have to keep up basic body functions. For me, that also consists of using an inspiratory spirometer. I've got to keep those lungs expanded. I never heard from my donor's family. I wonder how that person, whoever they were, in the next world, feels about me now.

The news reports that many are dying at the New Orleans airport for lack of hospital supplies. That's probably where they would have airlifted me. At the convention center, many had to leave their belongings because there wasn't room on the bus. They boarded the buses, making their way through the dead bodies. The rebuilding is to be called Project Hope. I've always said now that I've given up hope; I feel much better. For me, I see two options. One, move to Jefferson Parish; I don't see leaving the area entirely. Or two, bulldoze the rental property and use it to enjoy my family. Alexandra, the gal with the pit bulls, has run out of gas for her motorcycle. She is monitoring calls and she reports a lot of gunfire. Hope the National Guard arrives soon. A couple of people are feeding the roaming cats and dogs. Keep up the good work!

It's 2:00, the beginning of the bad time, meaning that it's hot and will be that way until at least 10:00 PM. I peer out the window and see a dragonfly go by. They're talking more about the looting and burning. I put my extra materials out of sight. If they get here, maybe they'll miss stuff. Now I just have to remember where things are. They mention that the people who stole an Abita water truck have been apprehended.

More choppers this afternoon. Some very slow moving; not sure what they seek to accomplish as this area is abandoned.

I have to talk about Critter. He was my client and a very scary individual. He was the strongest man I ever met. He could pick up a stove by himself and carry it a distance. When he first came to town I thought, here comes the Hell's Angels. He stayed and was very gruff, but he did adopt a pup, a Labrador mix. At around four months, the dog got a broken front leg—a nasty fracture that involved the elbow joint. Critter had minimum finances, so I splinted the leg and told him that the joint would probably freeze, but at a decent angle. In time, after the splint came off, the dog used the leg almost normally and after that, I was Critter's friend. He helped me with some moving and brute strength projects like hauling dirt. He still occasionally tangled with the law. In an argument, he broke his girlfriend's jaw. He once ran into my clinic bleeding after having been knifed in a bar fight. I bandaged his arm up, no charge. In the end, he was killed doing a drug deal down in the projects. Someone put a small headstone in the local park with his name. What a character—a lot of potential and little to show for it.

I'm sure glad I sent my dog with the family. I was thinking of keeping Sasha, a seven-year-old Samoyed female, here with me. She would have been miserable in the heat even though she was shaved down. I wouldn't have had food for her. I may have had to shoot her, and I might as well do the same for myself if that happened. She belonged to a client who was a carpenter. She would go to job sites. If she didn't, she would break out of her apartment and go beg for sandwiches at Igor's, a bar on St. Charles. She got sick, badly sick, every so often. Usually it was lead poisoning from the dirt from the paint on these old houses. She would lick the front of her legs constantly. The last time he brought her in, he owed me money so I never thought I'd see him again. But the owner of Igor's was footing the bill. He asked if I wanted her and, after turning down all sorts of offers for ten years, I said yes. She is the greatest. She's not super-bright, but very loving. She even came to see me at the hospital. When my family was leaving town, I looked around for her, and she was behind me, sitting there. I'll always remember that picture. Love you, Sashie-bear.

It's 3:00 PM. The sun is out, but there is a pall over the area. Perhaps it is from the smoke dissipating from the fires down on the waterfront. I fear fire more than water. One time I burned down an abandoned worm shed in a driving, torrential rain. Once I got that fire started, there was no stopping it. I've always been a bit of a pyromaniac. I liked burning debris; we cleared a lot of brush from borders on our farm. We also burnt a couple of old buildings. It's a tremendous force, one that always bears watching. It can reduce your treasures to ashes. Yet, it provides light. In the upcoming month, I don't wish to be its witness.

Some very heartwarming stories on the news. The Gumbo Crew is operating full force, serving meals. The Ecstasy, Sensation, and Holiday have been lined up for six months to provide housing for New Orleanians. The secretary of defense is going to visit, and the president should return on Monday. Saint Tammany Parish is not allowing any alcohol in the shelters as of six o'clock. That makes sense. I'm getting up after a nap; it is now 4:30 PM.

The newsmen make the point that the service/community workers have been working unceasingly. They are heroes. They also make the point that cellular phones are antennas on battlefields. Communication is poor. Deke, as well as Jerry V, said that you should share your thoughts with people. Just talking to someone is uplifting. There was a great story out of Jefferson Parish about a fellow who got in touch with a councilman here. His brother had not evacuated from 3409 Severn. The councilman went to the apartments and found four people. He let the brothers talk via a cell phone. He also got MREs and water for the survivors. Uplifting!

Price gauging is going on. They report sales of milk at $9.00 a gallon. There was another story about a couple renting an apartment. It went from $700 a month to $1,350 a month while they stood there. They say that price gauging is the same as looting. Would I do it if it were open to me? No.

A quick story. When parvo first started, the vaccine was hard to get. We even used feline vaccine because there was a cross-immunity. Although I heard prices went as high as $60 for a shot in New York City, I never charged higher than $8, and I could use every bit of vaccine. One veterinarian in the DC area did a very smart thing. He bought all the available mink vaccine (it also had cross-immunity), and then "leaked" the "news" of the disease to the media. All the other veterinarians quickly ran out of product, and he made a killing. Legitimate, yes. Ethical? Questionable. Goes to show that even in my profession, which is in the top three of most trusted professions along with pharmacy and nursing, there are some bad apples. I find a dead cockroach in my hall as I start my evening walk.

Eli and Peyton Manning have come down to help hand out supplies. This is very uplifting to the recipients. I wonder how much the NFL personnel will contribute. I've always wondered this prior to this disaster. When I took my mom to Touro Hospital the last time, I saw a gigantic man. I wondered who he was. His calves were as big as my thighs. I wonder how he's making out. I wonder.

I think about my friend, Nick. He moved to Waveland, Mississippi. Another cat person, he was right in the middle of the hurricane. When we first met him, he wouldn't give us his name because he thought that we would put him on a "list" and pester him. He's Buddhist; I wonder what his take is on all of this now. If I could get him on the cell phone, he would talk my head off, and I'd love it. He had a cat named Chester who was hurt badly in the back end. He had a broken femur and no tail function, but he was a scrapper. After weeks, that cat walked again. He died sometime afterward on the streets. Nick never gave up on him. Hang in there, Nick. I'm not giving up on you. I'm thinking about you and smiling.

Good news—the water in the commode is clear. That toilet probably hadn't been flushed for a month. That means standing water can be potable. Dinner was five crackers, six nuts, a small glass of decarbonated Sprite, and some water. Funny thing about those nuts. It's a large container from Sam's Club. I took every pecan out of them just prior to the storm to make an autumn nut cake. After I baked it, I painted cognac over the cake. I wish I had some of it right here, right now. Hey, I wonder if you can eat a Zulu coconut.

Somehow, it's cooler to sit here on a towel than on the sheets on my bed. It's 6:00 PM. I miss you, Katherine and Adriana.

They say a morgue in St. Gabriel is expected to get about 2,000 bodies. A black lady, who was evidently at the convention center, pronounces that she's a U.S. citizen, had been in New Orleans her whole life, and doesn't want to live there anymore. Texas has 125,000 people in ninety-seven shelters, and they need help. They have an additional 100,000 evacuees in hotels. The History Channel advertises about the series, "Rome." Cruise ships will be rerouted to Galveston and Mobile and not New Orleans. Too bad, but I understand the logistics. The Internet is functional in some areas, especially Yahoo and Craigslist.com. Someone called in to tell the folks about Richard Fitzgerald, a sixty-two-year-old who worked at the convention center. It was too dangerous for him to stay there. He walked to the Greater New Orleans Bridge and was turned back. He walked back to his apartment at 1313 Coliseum Street. Now these folks, who were in Amite, made contact with the radio station. He hears gunshots but is okay except he's a little nauseated. The broadcast goes on to ask about loved ones and gives out telephone numbers. I'd hate to think about how many people are waiting to use this service; kudos, once again, to WWL.

Gotta write this one down. Yesterday, I heard the radio say the people were lined up for buses at the Superdome. People would not get out of line and would urinate on themselves. The stench was unbelievable. One guy said that his sister was having a miscarriage and was asked to point her out. He would not get out of line to do that because he did not want to lose his spot. The gangs were roaming in the Superdome. Tourists would huddle in groups to stay safe. People were getting raped. Bodies were being rolled out (for the press). A woman had seizures on a sidewalk. Babies had cracked lips from dehydration.

Casey McCormick, a CBS radio professional reporter, interviewed some looters. She said that they were not proud of it, but they did it. Some soldiers that specialize in looking for snipers have come. Right now, there is no activity in this regard. The reporter talks about things being so surreal, saying the scenes in the "war zone" seemed like they were in another country. She couldn't believe that the scenes were in this country. I visualize Haiti. They talked about a patient airlifted to Huntsville, Alabama. He was eighty-four with bone cancer; sounds like money to me.

It's around 7:30 PM. I tried reading more about health. I'm stuck in the *B*s: beans, berries, and buckwheat. It's so hot, it's hard to concentrate. Standing is the coolest thing. I see a ripple outside my northerly window. There are some bubbles—very few. There was an old line in that section of the backyard, but we never cut it open. We've been here since 1992. We took comfort in knowing that the house next door never flooded and was built in the early 1950s. Never say never. There's also a noise, seemingly on the roof. Must be a squirrel, the sacred cow of New Orleans. They eat the pine nuts so he has some food. I mentally urge him to visit a neighbor's house. He can travel by wire. All is quiet. Time for Deke.

Sunday, September 4, 2005

I am awakened by chopper activity. There weren't as many of them last night. I had restless legs last night, but that was my fault because I drank some Coke to relieve a headache. The headache stopped, and in time, so did the restless legs. It got cooler earlier. I thought I would be comfortable by 8:30 PM, which is usually when I open the long window to its fullest extent. Someone was playing a game. It got cool, and then it got hot again until midnight when it wasn't bad at all. In the early hours, I actually had to get under a sheet. Let's see, five days now without clothes. Positively Neanderthal. I won't go on with any more description of myself.

I listened to the news again last night. There were some new broadcasters, perhaps one named Applebee. There's been more price gauging: $3.59 for a gallon of gas and $12.00 for a four-pack of D batteries. I guess these folks will get their way now, but in time, they too can be dealt with.

When I worked in Maryland, we had two poodles come in for surgery. They belonged to two different families. One dog had come in for a tail amputation, the other for a dental. Number two dog was knocked out and the tail shaved. Fortunately, the error was caught at that point. That evening, the irate owner insisted that we not charge him for any service and pay for three subsequent groomings. My boss agreed. Some time later, that same fellow brought the dog back for an eye problem. It had a growth on the third eyelid, a membrane that dogs have that comes from the medial side of the eye. It is not the eyeball. To take it out would mean picking it up, clamping, and cutting it, which would take a minute. We increased our fee to cover the previous losses. Unfortunately, for the dog, the growth was lymphosarcoma, which was bad news because it probably had traveled elsewhere. The forces of nature had caught up with the poodle's owner. I'll never forget that. So, be kind to your fellow man or everything can backfire.

This morning is a big day. I get to eat a can of beans. I have one for next Sunday too. I have sponged off this morning and brushed my teeth. On inspecting the battlements, the water level has gone down another six inches. The water is now taking on a slight tinge of green. The crows call. I heard a dog last night. It was probably down at the school, south of here, for protection. Sounded like a Rottweiler. He didn't bark for long. No cat. No Ed. It is sunny. We still have a slight breeze.

It's a little after 8:00 AM. There is a chopper that seems to be picking up something at the Fillmore overpass. He is down to the tree level and is hovering. Wonder how much gas it takes to operate one of them. The beans are pretty good. Garçon, some bread, please. Sorry, monsieur, we have only Triscuits. Will they do? Perfect, thank you. I have four Triscuits with my beans and pills and a little Coke. I am getting low on some of the pills; however, the antirejection drugs are in good shape. I lower the B12, the calcium, and the prednisone. The prednisone is for rejection but some folks exist on none. I drop from two every day to two every other day, interspersed with one. I eat only half of my beans, saving the rest for lunch.

Excuse me, there's someone banging on my roof, and it's not Santa Claus.

◆   ◆   ◆

I'm sitting here at Our Lady of the Lakes Hospital in Baton Rouge. I'm in the emergency room, having been helicoptered in from New Orleans. I want to remember what happened, so I'm going to flashback a couple of hours.

I opened the blinds on the northern side of the house and saw a fellow in a canoe. It was Joe Barrios, a surgeon from New Iberia. He and John Bordes were sent to get me by—you guessed it—my father-in-law. They said that my wife was frantic. I believe that! I told them that I was ready to go and asked how he wanted to get me. I initially handed my two bags out the southern window and was going to go out that way, but the canoe was not very steady. We decided that I should go out the northerly window. I'd have to break it out. I threw a five-pound exercise dumbbell through the window, knocked the rest out with a soup ladle, and put a blanket over the remaining chards of glass. I tied the rope to the bed. Joe gave me some gloves. I handed down my boots and then shinnied out the window. The bars that protected the lower half proved useful in giving me something to hang on to. He had given me a small life jacket to put on.

When I was successfully in the boat, I sat down and kept quiet. We negotiated our way between the houses. There were two anoles living in the vegetation at the top of my porch. I wished them luck. We went out on to Orleans Avenue, and it was disheartening. I saw two basketballs, my sport. I'll play again. We got to Fillmore and Orleans, and I notice the overpass over the canal is dry. I disembarked.

Another person was rescued in another boat. It's Bob—Robert Lee—a neighbor in the block to the south of us. He is in bad shape.

Bob's house was not two stories. To survive, he had to break into a neighbor's house. All of his dogs, an old Golden and two Bostons, were dead. He looked sallow. He is a diabetic (80 units/day) and used his last yesterday. He had nothing to eat. When I saw him, he did not recognize me at first. Of course, I haven't combed my hair in a week and I have facial hair, but he caught on within a few seconds. They put him on a gurney. I offered him an apple, and he gets a few bites. I was beginning to feed him some sirloin burger when they called to get him transported.

We traversed across the top of the overpass to the opposite bank of the canal. The whole area is full of water—I can't see where the road or lake was. The helicopter made a tremendous amount of wind. It looked like the hurricane was disturbing the water once again. Joe helped to hold me in one place as we crouched down, facing away from the helicopter. They loaded the stretcher, but I wasn't watching because I was protecting my eyes. When it was my turn, I went up with one of the soldiers.

Man, is it noisy. I had one chopper ride in the Army. We were at Camp Bullis, near San Antonio, in the early 70s. My group had successfully completed a course through the scrub and, in fact, the four of us were the first back to base. For that we got a copter ride. We were strapped in and there were no doors. As we were riding around, blissfully looking at the countryside, the pilots cut the power (for a second). I thought I'd die. When they cut it back on, after dropping several feet, we had our hearts in our mouths. They did it to everybody, but they all knew it was coming. We didn't. But I digress…

I went to the far side of the chopper. There were two pilots, one communications fellow, and two paramedics, Isaiah and Joe P. Bordes and Barrios climbed aboard. When we went up, I saw the flooding. It was very sad. The museum and sculpture garden were dry. We let Bordes and Barrios off at that point and headed for Baton Rouge.

I viewed the Cities of the Dead; half of the area was underwater. The railroad bridge on the I-10 at the new pumping station was under water from the beginning of the station to the sign that tells one to break off for Metairie Road.

We proceeded west. It was sunny; Metairie was dry. I spotted Lowe's on Veterans. That means Adriana's place is okay, I think. I can't be sure. Most of the roofs looked good; I only saw one house shattered (in the middle of many others that were seemingly untouched). The airport was clear, and then we were over the marsh. I saw one small house along a canal. It was totaled—it must have been a wildlife and fisheries station. There were some vehicles going down I-10 toward New Orleans.

Bob was being tended to. They got an IV going with NaCl in the drip. They used an Infusor, a squeeze bag, to move things along. I used to use those to give subcutaneous fluids to cats. I smile and pat Bob's knee. He is resting. The helicopter vibrates so much that his belly quivers. He's a big guy, somewhat overweight. It seems his legs are swollen, and I worry about that. I kept the apple.

The paramedic named Joe kept me abreast of my itinerary. We were five minutes away from touchdown in Baton Rouge when I saw a McDonald's. Maybe I'll get that hamburger sooner than I thought. I saw the state capitol and that large refinery north of the capitol. We touched down on top of the hospital and two doctors came out. After a brief conference, we are off again. They must have figured that Bob was too sick for their facility.

We land at Lady of the Lakes. Bob is taken off. Joe P. then comes for me. When I stood up, I'm a little unsteady. He takes my arm. By the time I'm out of the helicopter's wind, I'm okay. They triage me and determine that I don't have to be admitted. I agree. It'll be a waiting game. A nurse named Gina asks me if I need anything. I say I'm okay. They ask for my ID and hospital insurance card at admissions. Again, it is determined that I don't need to be admitted. I am in a lot better shape than the rest. A nurse brings me a sandwich and an orange juice with ice. Boy, that ice tastes great. I get to call my in-laws. The recording is on so I left a message. Now I will sit and wait. I hear a report that the emergency room is being readied for four officers that have been shot. I hope that's not true.

My wife's aunt and uncle have found me. I was sitting in the pediatric area because there were a bank of phones in that section. I initially heard from my daughter and her aunt (my wife's sister, Sarah). They were glad to hear from me. Evidently, the whole parish was looking for me. The rescuers came by twice but did not identify themselves so I did not communicate with them. It was good to see Aunt Donna and Uncle Adrian. They retired to Baton Rouge from New Jersey in 1990. The area has grown rapidly. However, not as fast as in the last week—a city of 250,000 gaining 100,000 people in one week. They have to figure out what to do with these folks. I am lucky; my wife's family base is in New Iberia, but there are many relatives scattered throughout the state. Right now, my father-in-law, Doug, is helping his youngest daughter, Andre, clear trees around her house in Mandeville. That area has a lot of pines and one has hit the house. Edward, the son of Sarah (who is the oldest daughter), is helping clear trees also.

Aunt Donna and Uncle Adrian stayed with me for an hour. We talked about the happenings in Baton Rouge, the looting, the efforts of the federal government to help. I listened to the problems of Mississippi. I heard some of Wolf Blitzer. Thankfully, it was a kids' area and someone changed the channel. Everyone wants to blame somebody. Yes, there are some blamable things and there will be investigations, but what happened to being prepared and self-reliant? Yes, you can say that I have the family to back me up. I have to ask each of you pointing a finger, what good is it? How prepared are you, and where are you going? What's your plan? The finger points at you too. Instead of grousing, what are you doing about your problems?

I've been alone before. I once left Florida with nothing. I did have a profession, so I had what was in my head. It was very discouraging to be later cut down by my respiratory problem. Then I spent a little over a month in the hospital fixing that back in October 2003. I was almost done in this time except for handling my ring and my daughter's bracelet. We are going to rebuild in New Orleans as a family.

Now I'm on my way to New Iberia. It's sunny, and guess what—the car is air-conditioned.

Epilogue

I went back to the house again today. I go because I seek to retrieve things that I think I will find in good shape. Of course, nothing is in good shape. It's disheartening.

It's been eleven weeks since the rescue, but it seems like that helicopter ride was only a short time ago. My family is doing okay, although the canine invasion at my in-laws has not been without its trials. My dog Sasha, for instance, likes to go swimming in the goldfish pond and that is a definite no-no.

My daughter is doing well in school in New Iberia and is expected to get back to Benjamin Franklin High School in January 2006. The school has received charter status. One sad note is that one of her wheelchairs was left at the school and was not salvageable.

My wife is a little stressed, but who isn't? Her office building had a foot of water for thirty-six hours. Then, the parish started the pumps back up again, and the water went away. We were not allowed to see her business for two weeks. We then fought the mold and other things. Friends came by to help us clean and rebuild. We pulled sheet rock and base cabinets, met with insurance adjusters, fixed the roof, cleaned up debris, and managed her business from 135 miles away. Next week, we'll almost be back to normal and that's doing well! I have lived above the clinic for at least the last month—time slips away. Guess I like second-story living.

Our house is a deserted lady. She has mold on the ceilings. She is black inside; the kitchen cabinets have fallen. Our furniture floated around, landed in different rooms, and then fell apart. All of my music—I played guitar—is gone. I sifted through some papers and could separate them to get necessary items secured, like the title to the property. The pool is black and full of duckweed. All of the vegetation is brown except for the crepe myrtle, an occasional oak, and some weeds. Even my safety deposit box at the local bank flooded.

My neighbors are not there. Brad has recovered from the pancreatitis, and their second child is doing fine. My accountant's brick house shifted on its pilings and will have to be demolished. Our house will also have to be demolished because we have to elevate our living area eight to ten feet, being below the flood plain. FEMA has helped, the Red Cross has helped, and my insurance companies have helped. I appreciate their efforts. Even Garland Robinette on WWL, by crusading for better schools and guided government spending, has won my respect.

Yet everything is so dead in Lakeview. There is no electrical power or telephone service. We do have water pressure. There is still a curfew. We are moving into a small rental house in Metairie, which we were lucky to get. It's from a lady vet who used to work for me—a kind of a total financial reversal, you might say.

Anyway, we'll go on. It'll be months before we know it and hopefully the spring will give us a welcome greening to our land. The upcoming holiday season should help brighten our spirits and outlook. I wish, though, we were back home.

Happy Holidays!

978-0-595-38191-3
0-595-38191-X